Freedom of Speech and Society

Freedom of Speech and Society

A Social Approach to Freedom of Expression

Harry Melkonian

Cambria Press

Amherst, New York

Requests for permission should be directed to
permissions@cambriapress.com, or mailed to:
Cambria Press
University Corporate Center, 100 Corporate Parkway, Suite 128
Amherst, NY 14226

Library of Congress Cataloging-in-Publication Data

Melkonian, Harry.
Freedom of speech and society: a social approach
to freedom of expression / Harry Melkonian.
p. cm.
Includes bibliographical references and index
ISBN 978-1-60497-820-9 (alk. paper)
1. Freedom of speech—social aspects—United States. I. Title.

KF4772.M45 2012
323.44'30973—dc23

2012026267

In memory of my brothers, James and Jon

Table of Contents

List of Tables

Foreword

As I sit down to write this foreword, it is perhaps only fitting that I do so in the midst of America's quadrennial (and noisy) exercise in participatory democracy: the presidential election. The Republican National Convention in Tampa has just ended (with Mr. Mitt Romney anointed the party standard bearer), loyal Democrats will rally around President Barack Obama at their convention in Charlotte this week, and sixty-four days from now the country will head to the polls to elect a national leader. During this election cycle there will be talk, talk, and more talk. Impassioned speeches, attack ads, editorials, testimonials, talking heads, and twitter mania; insistent e-pleas for contributions to keep it all going; and, of course, charges and countercharges that the other side is bending the facts to secure the election.[1] Political factions and interest groups abound, all speaking and writing and texting their conflicting views at the same time, all covered by a ubiquitous media that reports, polls and analyzes 24/7. And from this cacophony of free speech—this "uninhibited, robust and wide-open" debate[2]—majoritarian consensus, perhaps even truth, will emerge.

Or so the theory goes.

For centuries, writers, philosophers and, more recently, jurists and law professors have expounded differing theories on why free expression is essential in an enlightened society. From the constitutive approach of the ancient Greeks and Immanuel Kant (that free speech is an intrinsic good unto itself that furthers individual self-fulfillment) to the instrumental justifications of John Stuart Mill (free speech furthers the search for truth), Oliver Wendell Homes (free speech fosters a "marketplace" of competing ideas) and Professor Alexander Meiklejohn (free speech is necessary for informed self-government), not to mention Spinoza, Alexis de Tocqueville, or feminist analysis, the canon of free speech theory is crowded indeed. Can anything new possibly be said?

This is where Dr. Harry Melkonian's fascinating book, *Freedom of Speech and Society: A Social Approach to Freedom of Expression*, enters the fray. In this book, Dr. Melkonian departs from the more-traditional philosophical, political and individual justifications for free speech and examines freedom of expression through the lens of sociology—and, more specifically, the causal sociology of the nineteenth-century thinker Emile Durkheim and the modern writings of Jurgen Habermas. Whereas traditional free speech theories seek to explain why people *should* have freedom of expression (to promote individual dignity, or ascertain truth or effectively govern ourselves), Dr. Melkonian employs social science to answer a more fundamental question: Why *is* freedom of expression typically the norm in modern, industrial democracies? As Dr. Melkonian posits below:

> "Freedom of expression is both a cause and a consequence of social systems. It is a function of individualization caused by the division of labor in society. Sociology may not explain the virtues of free speech but is more conclusionary—society requires it to function. As the group becomes a collection of autonomous beings fulfilling a more specific role, communication is essential or the social organism can no longer function."

Or to use my example, while individual freedom of expression in presidential elections (or railing against City Hall) surely brings about a rosy glow of self-fulfillment and furthers the goals of self-government, Dr. Melkonian—building on social theory—also views the very act of communicating differing views as a *cause* and *result* of complex democratic society—essential (and, hence, present) in democracies like America, the United Kingdom, or Japan; unnecessary (and, hence, absent) in totalitarian regimes such as North Korea. Dr. Melkonian does not so much reject traditional theories of free expression (although he does find logical shortcomings with some). Rather, he seeks to reorient our perspective—from philosophical to sociological.

While Dr. Melkonian employs a sociology framework, this is very much a book about the law, and free speech law in particular. Dr. Melkonian finds convincing validation for the role sociology plays in the evolution of free expression through, for example, a fascinating analysis of the demise of criminal libel laws in the United Kingdom and United States—correctly noting that, as countries like the United Kingdom and United States have moved from their agrarian past to complex industrial societies (in which communication of views is essential to societal cohesion), criminal libel has been replaced by the tort of civil libel as the appropriate remedy to balance speech and reputational interests. He also surveys the U.S. Supreme Court's First Amendment jurisprudence (and, indeed, the development of First Amendment doctrine and libel laws) through the unique prism of social theory. And while this is surely a book about big ideas, along the way Dr. Melkonian treats us to a colorful array of examples and supporting evidence that make this journey eminently enjoyable—including "tongue boring and limb breaking" (seventeenth-century punishments for libel), the murals of Diego Rivera, the middle finger, the Protestant Reformation, the Alien & Sedition Acts, and even the archeological digs at Catalhoyuk and Gobekli Tepe in Turkey.

Suffice it to say that, not unlike an archeologist, Dr. Melkonian seeks to reinterpret the shards of free expression development using the tools of sociology—and in the process offers a fresh perspective that challenges long-held orthodoxies. But enough. For a truly rewarding and original discussion of freedom of expression theory, one I know will inform and delight, I will now let Dr. Melkonian do the talking.

– Robert Balin
Partner and Media Practice Chair, Davis Wright Tremaine LLP, and Adjunct Professor, Columbia Law School

Endnotes

1. Or as The *New York Times* more tartly puts it, "[t]he growing number of misrepresentations appear to reflect a calculation in both parties that shame is overrated." Facts Take Beating in Acceptance Speeches, N.Y. Times, A13 (Aug. 31, 2012).

2. *New York Times v. Sullivan*, 376 U.S. 254, 270 (1964).

Preface

Why another book on freedom of speech? It is hardly the situation that the literature does not already have a large complement of current and classical works. My response to this rather obvious question begins with the observation that the traditional theories do not resolve all of the questions regarding freedom of expression and this is especially true with respect to United States Supreme Court interpretations of the First Amendment. Understanding freedom of expression is a work in progress, and new aspects seem to be continually emerging from the pens of legal philosophers. My intent was not to attempt a grand or unified theory that purports to explain everything concerning free speech and its restrictions, but rather I proceeded with the hope that this discussion could open new areas of inquiry, namely, exploration of the sociological or even anthropological traditions in addition to the more traditional legal and philosophical justifications for freedom of expression. In a nutshell, the central theme of this book is that free speech and its limitations are the natural and necessary consequences of social development in modern complex societies and that inappropriate restrictions or extensions of freedom of speech can hobble society itself by promoting unsustainable social disharmony.

From the perspective of traditional free speech analysis, this book reaches a rather surprising, if not radical, conclusion. Free speech theory has generally been divided into two types of justification: instrumental or constitutive. The instrumental theories state that freedom of expression is desirable to the extent that it helps to attain a particular goal—usually political, such as democracy—whereas the constitutive justifications argue that freedom of speech is desirable simply because free expression is part of individual liberty or autonomy, and its desirability does not depend on attaining specific goals. It should not be surprising that, within the realm of courts and legislators, the instrumental approach has gathered far more traction. In contrast to the traditional dichotomy of speech justifications, this book argues that all free speech falls within the instrumental justification because broad rights of freedom of expression extending beyond political speech are not just a matter of being morally desirable but are essential for the functioning of modern complex societies that exhibit extensive division of labour. To the extent that freedom of expression can be justified through an instrumental—as opposed to a constitutive—justification, the likelihood of judicial recognition may be enhanced as one moves from arguments that may be viewed as esoteric to positions that are concrete and pragmatic.

Virtually all existing free speech theories focus on the content of speech. Yet, in the United States the Supreme Court, having briefly accepted content as the linchpin for constitutionally protected speech, quickly returned to its initial perspective of attaching constitutional protection based on the status of the target of the speech—the so-called public figure. From the traditional free speech perspective, the American approach has led to a hodgepodge of rules that appear at odds with sound theory. However, once viewed through the lens of sociological theory, the American approach is not only reasonable but also harmonious with the sociology of speech. While not citing sociological theory, the US Supreme Court has a history of employing sociological information to decide constitutional issues and, as it turns out, this is also the case with the First Amendment.

Initially, this project was inspired by some research concerning the evolution and now-terminal state of criminal defamation law in the United States and the United Kingdom (where Parliament had finally seen fit to put this archaic doctrine out of its—and the publics'—misery). As I reviewed the historical record of the downward trend in criminal defamation cases, I was reminded of Emile Durkheim's earliest sociological theory developed in the late nineteenth century and his ideas about diminution in criminal sanctions with concomitant replacement with civil sanctions for the same occurrence as being a function of increasing division of labour and social complexity. Once having applied Durkheim's classical theory to criminal defamation and finding substantial validation, I was curious if a division of labour analysis could be pushed further and broadened to not just defamation law but also freedom of expression itself. The result is this book wherein I maintain that freedom of expression and restrictions on that freedom are the natural results of division of labour or, in Durkheim's words "organic solidarity" that flows from the division of labour.

To bring the classical sociology of Durkheim into the twenty-first century, I have employed some of Jurgen Habermas's communicative theory which complements earlier ideas. I have also taken this opportunity to develop more fully the continuing relevance of Durkheim's theories not only in the context of freedom of speech and criminal libel but also with respect to the very origins of civilisation itself. While somewhat afield from freedom of speech, the civilisation discussion is included to illustrate that Durkheim's theories continue to find new relevance and application in the social sciences. Finally, the book explores the relationship of sociological theory to the series of free speech decisions of the US Supreme Court beginning with *New York Times v. Sullivan* in 1964 and concludes that the American approach of focusing on the public or private status of the target of the speech, as opposed to the content of speech, embodies the sound influence of sociology on traditional free speech theory.

Although this book makes substantial reference to social theory, it is not a work intended for sociologists who might find the reliance on Durkheim somewhat quaint or dated nor is it intended as a contribution to sociological research. The text is more directed to members of the legal community and philosophers who are interested in freedom of expression and its justifications. Durkheim was selected because his classical theories are of continuing relevance and clearly stated and because his theory concerning social division of labour lends itself to being applied to freedom of expression.

There are constant social and political tensions calling for the expansion or contraction of rights to free expression. As centralised electronic data gathering of personal information expands, the threat to privacy begins to make even those of us not prone to conspiracy theories begin to border on paranoia. On one hand, acknowledging that the right to privacy is also a fundamental human right, freedom of expression cannot be without limits. On the other hand, in light of restrictions on speech as seen in many countries in the post 9/11 environment, caution must be taken in thinking that the need for security overcomes the right to freedom of expression. This discussion does not lend itself to easy answers because security, privacy, and freedom of speech are all matters of legitimate concern. As US Supreme Court Justice Arthur Goldberg observed in *Kennedy v. Mendoza-Martinez* (372 US 144, 161 [1963]), "while the Constitution protects against invasions of individual rights, it is not a suicide pact." A goal of this book is to offer a dispassionate explanation for the proposition that freedom of expression and appropriate limitations are essential to the existence and survival of large complex societies and that unfettered rights pose as great a societal peril as excessive restrictions.

My ambition is not to congest the free speech debate even further but rather to provide an intellectual mechanism for better reconciling freedom of speech with social values. While the actual text reflects research that I have conducted over the past five years, the underlying thought cannot be separated from the accumulated knowledge garnered from nearly forty years of practicing and teaching law in the United States and, more recently, Australia. I am grateful for this wealth of experience and it was with enormous effort that I refrained from punctuating arguments with the type of anecdotal material or war stories that lawyers love to dwell upon and which invariably bore listeners or readers.

Acknowledgments

I am indebted to Professors Denise Meyerson and Malcolm Voyce at Macquarie University Law School. During my PhD studies, Professor Meyerson, a highly regarded legal philosopher, was very supportive in my first foray into using social theory as a framework for a free speech analysis. While taking a postgraduate research course from Malcolm Voyce, I was re-acquainted with Max Weber, Emile Durkheim, and other social theorists. This brought me back intellectually to the heady days in the 1960s when I studied anthropology at the University of Rochester and became initiated with the theoretical world that so enervates university students when they first realise that the world is much more complex than they previously imagined. I hope that the free speech discussion in this book stimulates others to expand the argument and pursue it in new directions.

I am, of course, most grateful to my wife, Dr Wei Wu, and our boys Axel and Wyatt for their support and understanding. As for the days and nights of self-imposed sequestration where I reviewed and endured sociological theory from Durkheim to Habermas and tried to glean out pearls that might explain human communication and freedom of expression, special thanks must go to our two very patient dogs who were so happy just to share my company, poor as it may have been. Finally, I happily and respectfully dedicate this book to my two youngest brothers who sadly never had the opportunity to fully sample all that this world has to offer. Any errors of interpretation are purely my own.

Introduction

While highly valued in democratic societies, freedom of speech has never been an unfettered right. Speech is regulated through a large body of laws which cover a spectrum including defamation, privacy, pornography, political campaign contribution limits, broadcasting license regulations, and many others. This book evolved from an effort to reconcile some of the philosophical arguments that have been made for freedom of speech with the numerous and changing real-world restrictions on speech. While political and legal philosophers have crafted a corpus of rich literature in support of free speech, the acceptance of restrictions on speech indicates that other factors are influencing speech limits contrary to the broad and seemingly unrestricted arguments advanced by legal theorists. This text represents an attempt to introduce established social theory to the free speech debate with the hope that sociology might help to explain freedom of expression as it actually exists. Although it is necessary to introduce a limited amount of sociological terminology in this discussion, to maintain linguistic harmony with existing literature, discussion and comparisons of freedom of expression will be within the parameters or confines generally recognised by modern free speech theorists—constitutive and instrumental justifications, with the instrumental arguments for free speech being those that are results oriented and the constitutive theories being those that focus on the general emotional and intellectual well-being of individual citizens.

One could raise the point that freedom-of-speech literature is already so well populated by philosophers and legal scholars that there is not any reason to add another discipline such as sociology to the theoretical mix. In response, there are at least six reasons for sociological considerations. First, freedom of speech and its limits are an ongoing discourse. If sociology can make a contribution to the discussion, then the contribution should be welcome. Second, there seems to be a limitation in the philosophical arguments in support of freedom of speech—philosophers tend to speak in absolutes, and there is not any society that has ever accepted absolutes in freedom of speech. Even in ancient Athens, where debate and philosophy flourished, Socrates was executed for polluting the minds of the young with dangerous thoughts. Third, within the existing framework for analysing and advocating freedom of expression as between instrumental and constitutive justifications, sociological arguments provide a basis for recasting the more philosophical constitutive justification for free speech into the more results-oriented instrumental justification. Fourth, advocates for freedom of expression have typically spoken in terms of individual rights. However, beyond the individual, there exists society with its own rights and expectations. One of the greatest contributions of French sociologist Emile Durkheim was his ongoing dialogue with other social theorists who he believed failed to recognise that society was something other than a collection of individuals. In Durkheim's metaphor, individuals, as compared to society, were akin to organs within the human body; vital components but essentially different from the human organism. Durkheim further envisaged that all of the other social disciplines, such as philosophy and law, would form a pyramid of knowledge with sociology at the apex taking in and synthesising all of the other disciplines. While philosophers and legal scholars would likely take exception to this rather lofty view of sociology, it is arguably undisputed that sociological theory can make an important contribution in explaining human conduct. Fifth, sociology provides a theoretical foundation for the seemingly eccentric position of the US Supreme Court with respect to its focus on the public or private persona of the target of speech rather than on the content of the speech. Sixth, as discussed in the conclusion, freedom of speech now recognises a pluralistic approach admitting of many arguments and justifications. Sociological explanations further extend the pluralism and may even enlighten the ongoing debate. Finally, as a matter of legal symmetry, sociology, which has already been employed to describe the tort of defamation, should also be explored to see if it can also explain the countervailing arguments for freedom of speech.

From the beginnings of twentieth-century sociology, there have always been at least two general schools of thought regarding the nature of society. Max Weber built his theories around the concept that society could be understood as a collection or population of individuals interacting with each other. Durkheim, however, saw society as something decidedly distinct and different from its members. The constitutive justification for freedom of expression has usually been cast in the Weberian manner—all forms of freedom of speech are good for the full potential of the individual. The instrumental justification has typically been espoused on a more society-wide basis—freedom of speech on political matters helps to promote self-government or democracy. Central to the arguments presented in this book is the belief that the constitutive justification can be applied to society as a whole and not just the individual. Using theories drawn from Durkheim and contemporary social theorist Jurgen Habermas, it is suggested that freedom of speech is essential for society as a whole and as distinct from the individual. The full extension of this argument leads to the conclusion that all freedom of speech is instrumental (or results oriented) because it is required in order for a society as a whole to operate smoothly.

In addition to recasting constitutive theories or philosophic discussions into more means- or results-oriented arguments, a sociological approach may also be employed to describe freedom of speech (and its limitations) as it exists in any society at a specific time, as a function or creation of social forces and to that degree, as an inevitable aspect of the human social condition that does not necessarily require independent philosophical justification. Beyond justifying freedom of expression, a sociological approach furnishes an explanation for the reasons that the otherwise unfettered philosophical arguments for free speech must be tempered by other social values. Application of sociological theory can also lead to some startling results such as why freedom of speech in some societies not only is—but possibly should be—expected to be less than in others. While some philosophers in the tradition of John Stuart Mill may argue for unfettered freedom of speech, sociological theory can rationally insist that this individual freedom can be a destructive force unless it is interpreted within the parameters of healthy social existence. In other words, unrestricted freedom of expression may be fine for Robinson Crusoe living on his island, but once he meets up with his compatriot Friday, their collective happiness and well-being invoke values separate and distinct from what is required for the individual.

Freedom of speech or freedom of expression[1] has been justified and explained by notable political and legal philosophers including John Locke, Benedict Spinoza, John Milton, John Stuart Mill, Immanuel Kant, Alexander Meiklejohn, Zechariah Chafee, Jr., Thomas Emerson, and more recently by Lee Bollinger, Alan Haworth, Cass Sundstein, Eric Barendt, C Edwin Baker, Steven Heyman, Robert Hargreaves, Frederick Schauer, Owen Fiss, Anthony Lewis, Steven Shiffrin, Rodney Smolla, Ronald Dworkin, and many others of similar stature. These philosophers and legal scholars developed many convincing arguments why freedom of speech is desirable for individual development and satisfaction. The philosophers have tended to develop highly abstract normative concepts while legal scholars have tended to address free speech as something derived from constitutional and common law.[2]

Understanding freedom of speech in as many theoretical perspectives as possible plays a role in evaluating acceptable limitations. Governments are constantly proposing restrictions on freedom of speech through any number of ostensibly meritorious purposes such as eliminating child pornography or restricting television and radio licenses to responsible broadcasters. By expanding our knowledge of what freedom of speech is intended to achieve on both individual and societal levels, courts, legislators, and the public can more effectively evaluate proposals that would either expand or further restrict speech. For example, legal philosophers like Alexander Meiklejohn very clearly and convincingly articulated the role of free speech with respect to discussing and debating the merits of political matters in a democracy. His arguments present a formidable no-go zone for government regulation of the content of campaign speeches and commentary. While Professor Meiklejohn's arguments for freedom of speech were generally confined to the functioning of democratic governments, other free speech advocates, perhaps operating from a more purely philosophical base, such as John Stuart Mill and Immanuel Kant, presented far-ranging theories that admitted few limitations. However, while Mill and Kant provide broad theoretical arguments, their theories have not met with legal or judicial acceptance nearly as well as more pointed or goal-specific arguments such as those proposed by Meiklejohn.

In formulating many of the principles of sociology, Emile Durkheim was essentially at odds with the strident individualism advocated by John Stuart Mill, the nineteenth-century's foremost advocate of freedom of expression. Durkheim argued that unfettered individualism was destructive of society and that individual rights had to be restrained by societal interests.[3] The interests of society as opposed to individualism form a central theme in this text. While sociological theory has clearly progressed subsequent to Durkheim, his classical texts continue to represent valid and clear theory in the same way that Isaac Newton's classical laws of physics remain important even in the age of Einstein.

One of the countervailing values to freedom of expression is the right to reputation protected by privacy and defamation laws that include the torts of invasion of privacy, breach of confidence, libel, and slander.[4]

The tension between the right of freedom of expression and the right to protect human reputation through defamation and privacy laws is an ongoing discourse. Different societies have reached different balances as perhaps exemplified by the extremely strict common law libel regime in Australia as opposed to the preference for freedom of speech found in modern US Supreme Court interpretations of the First Amendment to the US Constitution. The relevance of defamation law as a component of the free speech debate has received considerable scholarly attention in recent years from legal experts including Michael Chesterman, Andrew Kenyon, Paul Mitchell, David Rolph, Lawrence McNamara, Dario Milo, Ian Cram, Roy Baker, Anthony Lewis, and Ian Loveland among others.

An unusual aspect of defamation law is that it is an essentially sociological tort. This argument was raised in a seminal article by Robert Post published in 1986 entitled "The Social Foundations of Defamation Law: Reputation and the Constitution."[5] More recently, Ian Cram has raised cultural and historical considerations for variations in the balance between freedom of expression and legal restrictions on speech in variations liberal democracies.[6] Essentially, defamation is a sociological tort because it allows an individual to recover damages for injury to reputation in the eyes of others. However, not only is defamation a sociological tort but freedom of speech can also be described sociologically and thereby cultural or sociological factors can be used in balancing freedom of expression with other rights such as right to reputation. A sociological approach to freedom of speech offers an explanation for the differing levels of acceptance of traditional free speech theories in different societies. For example, Canada and the United States are democracies with popularly elected local, regional, and national governments, and the courts in both countries have recognised Professor Meiklejohn's democracy-based free speech theory. Nevertheless, the United States rather clearly promotes freedom of speech concerning political matters to a greater degree than the equally democratic Canada. Does this reflect a flaw in Canada's application of free speech theory? Professor Cram has suggested that it does not and instead reflects different Canadian cultural values.[7] Accepting the role of local cultural traditions as influencing freedom of speech, the door is open to introducing sociological theory to inform the dialogue that seeks to reconcile sometimes conflicting rights and interests.

In general, like philosophy, sociological theory is neither definitively correct nor incorrect. Instead, it seeks to explain social behaviour and, like philosophy, various theories coexist in harmony. The arguments in this book will centre on a basic sociological concept that Durkheim believed could explain many aspects of society, namely, the division of labour in society. Durkheim derived a great deal of his ideas from observing the social division of labour found in almost all aspects of modern social life in industrial societies. More recently, Jurgen Habermas's extensive writing on discourse and communicative theory in the context of modern European society is equally revealing and also establishes the need for both respect and freedom of expression in order for society to function. Habermas extended Durkheim's arguments by adding the concept that freedom of expression also requires that the speaker be taken seriously by listeners. This argument dovetails into some contemporary arguments concerning human dignity that are normally considered within the constitutive justification for freedom of speech.

At its core, this book will utilise social theory to argue that freedom of expression and its limitations are the natural consequences of division of labour and that the division of labour in society requires freedom of expression. Perhaps the major departure from the philosophical tradition is the argument that freedom of speech, including restrictions necessary for social harmony, is inevitable in contemporary social environments and that without appropriately balanced rights to freedom of expression, society would be impaired.

Philosophy and law encompass far more than freedom of expression and, similarly, sociological theory has an extensive and growing body of literature that ranges over many aspects of the human condition. Within the universe of sociological theorists, only those who dealt with communication were suitable for this work. Two sociologists were selected—

one classical and the other contemporary—but both are very theoretical and the latter drawing from the former. Emile Durkheim was chosen to represent the classical tradition and Jurgen Habermas the contemporary perspective. Adding sociological theory to philosophy is not quite as radical as it may seem because it is sometimes difficult to separate the sociologist from the political or legal philosopher. While Emile Durkheim is generally accepted as a sociologist and not a philosopher, once discussion turns to figures such as contemporary German social theorist Jurgen Habermas, it is somewhat murkier—is he a sociologist or philosopher? Given that free speech texts rarely, if ever, include Habermas in discussions or anthologies, Habermas will be usurped into the role of sociologist because the free speech philosophers have not yet taken him into their fold publicly. Habermas has created a still-unfinished colloquy concerning freedom of expression. As did Durkheim, Habermas writes prolifically and also occupies a high status within the ranks of sociological theorists. Clearly other sociologists could have been selected, but the choice of Durkheim and Habermas were not arbitrary. Durkheim is generally regarded as the founder of modern sociology and created much of the early theory that continues to guide sociological thought. Durkheim's early writing on the role of the division of labour in society is readily transferable into a discussion of human communication. For a contemporary contribution, Jurgen Habermas, who has written extensively about communicative theory and the human condition in general, seemed a logical choice.

Politically, Durkheim and Habermas are perhaps strange bedfellows. Durkheim rejected Marx because Durkheim saw religion as the primary moving force in human society whereas Marx viewed political economy in the same role.[8] Durkheim also condemned the role of sociologist as a moving force or revolutionary but maintained that sociologists, to be true to their calling, must only be observers. Habermas, in contrast, has a more varied intellectual history and his political philosophy has undergone metamorphosis or maturation as his theories continue to evolve. Initially, he was substantially influenced by Marxism but, with the passage of time, he has travelled far afield intellectually from those early influences and today his writing may be more reflective of the tradition of Durkheim.[9] Habermas has also chosen to be involved actively in German and European Union affairs and has eschewed Durkheim's tenet of being an uninvolved observer.

The sociological arguments concerning free speech will be presented before more traditional legal philosophy is considered. This approach has been taken to demonstrate the ability of the sociological theories to stand independently of philosophical justifications. After a recapitulation of some of the philosophy of free speech, an attempt will be made to amalgamate or at least harmonise the two and show how the constitutive justification for freedom of expression, through the use of sociological theory, becomes distinctly instrumental or results oriented.

ENDNOTES

1. Freedom of speech and freedom of expression will be used interchangeably.
2. See generally, D. Richards, "Free Speech as Toleration" in W Waluchow (ed) *Free Expression,* 31–57.
3. Ken Morrison, *Marx Durkheim Weber–Formations of Modern Social Thought,* 153–155.
4. As the distinctions between libel and slander have largely disappeared, libel, slander, and defamation will be used interchangeably.
5. Robert Post, "The Social Foundations of Defamation Law: Reputation and the Constitution", *California Law Review* 74 (1986): 691.
6. Ian Cram, *Contested Words: Legal Restrictions on Freedom of Speech in Liberal Democracies,* 31–41.
7. Ibid., 31–32.
8. Emile Durkheim, *The Rules of Sociological Method.* Translated by W. D. Walls, 167–174.
9. See Ruth Wallace and Alison Wolf, *Contemporary Sociological Theory,* 174–175.

FREEDOM OF SPEECH
AND SOCIETY

Chapter 1

The Nature of Speech and Freedom of Speech

Before considering appropriate parameters for freedom of expression, it is necessary to define the activity that is to be protected. While many forms of human activity that constitute speech are very clear, there are areas where the definition is by no means self-evident.[1] Activities such as conversations, print in all forms, broadcasts, film, video, dramatic performances, recordings, and all electronic communications are clearly speech in the conventional sense; sometimes physical activity or conduct that communicates a message also amounts to speech. Artistic works frequently have a strong speech component and may in fact be very powerful when subjects include sculpture such as the Statue of Liberty in New York harbour.[2] Since most conduct contains some element of communication, distinctions must be drawn or the legal concept of speech loses all meaning. For example, a punch in the nose clearly communicates displeasure and a bank robbery communicates a desire for money; yet neither of these activities falls within the legal concept of speech. It is still a matter of unresolved debate in the United States whether the so-called "middle-finger salute" constitutes protected speech or prosecutable disorderly conduct. However the clear trend seems to be in favour of the middle digit as speech.[3]

In 2006, the US Supreme Court had occasion to review the nature of speech in *Rumsfeld v. Forum for Academic and Institutional Rights, Inc.*[4] This case involved a claim of constitutionally protected free speech by some of America's most prestigious law schools. The case was inherently political and emotional and was charged with claims of Eastern elitism and disparagement of the American defence forces. A group of law schools, all belonging to major universities and opposed to the discriminatory policy then pursued by the military against gays, barred military recruiters from using law school facilities for interviewing students who wanted to inquire about opportunities for lawyers in the defence forces. The law schools maintained that by granting the military access to on-campus interviewing facilities, the law schools would be victims of compelled speech; that is, they would be viewed as expressing support for the military's discriminatory policies.

The dispute arose over the response of Congress to the exclusion of the military recruiters from the law schools. In the aftermath of the exclusions, Congress enacted the *Solomon Amendment*[5] which cut off all government funding to any university (not just law schools where federal funding is possibly *de minimis*) in which the military did not enjoy the same recruiting privileges as other prospective employers. To anticipate First Amendment issues relating to the free exercise of religion clause of the First Amendment, an exception was made for universities that had an established history of pacifism based on the religious affiliation of the school. While law schools could likely survive the threatened loss of funding, the consequence of medical schools or science departments being cut off from federal funds was something that no major university could possibly risk. The universities asserted that the *Solomon Amendment* was unconstitutional as it amounted to coerced speech, thereby forcing the schools to endorse the anti-gay discrimination. The law schools were unsuccessful at the trial court[6] but prevailed at the Third Circuit Court of

Appeals and the law was struck as violating the First Amendment.[7] On review, a unanimous Supreme Court disagreed, declared the law constitutional, and addressed the issue of when conduct could be considered as speech. The Court noted that the *Solomon Amendment* did not restrict the law schools from placing signs on the wall saying that they did not approve of military policies nor were protests banned. The only conduct required by the law was equal access to interview facilities.

The law schools were correct and on solid ground in asserting that compelled speech can be just as repugnant to freedom of speech as repressed or censored speech. There is a freedom not to permit the state to intrude on individual or group political beliefs and religious associations.[8] The Supreme Court agreed that precedents clearly established that the government could not force children to say the pledge of allegiance in schools;[9] the government could not require people to use license registration plates that bore state mottos offensive to them, specifically in the case of New Hampshire where registration plates bear the motto "Live Free or Die";[10] and could not outlaw the burning of American flags.[11] Nevertheless, the court distinguished these activities because in all of those cases, the conduct complained of was clearly and plainly expressive whereas the provision of interview rooms was so far removed from communicating a message that the law schools had to publish notices explaining why they were excluding military recruiters. The Supreme Court said that "nothing about recruiting suggests that law schools agree with any speech by recruiters, and nothing in the Solomon Amendment restricts what the law schools may say about the military's policies."[12]

While perhaps a closer question than the unanimous Supreme Court vote implied, the *Rumsfeld* case on its face appeared to be different from the ban on the flag burning situation where the law sought to outlaw inherently expressive conduct. Of course, the public burning of the US flag is not only expressive conduct but is also highly emotional. Flag burning, having been found to constitute protected speech has resulted in attempts, unsuccessful to date, to amend the Constitution to specifically prohibit the activity.[13] The issue is so emotional that even after the Supreme Court decision in 1990, flag burning and desecration continues to be an emotional issue in the US and local governments continued to prosecute offenders even though the charges invariably failed either at trial or on appellate review.[14] While public incineration of the American flag communicates an unambiguous and powerful message, in *Rumsfeld*, the expressive aspect of barring military recruiters was found to be simply too attenuated for the conduct to be protectable speech.[15] As the court also observed, to permit such an interpretation of speech would enable others who disagree with military policies to simply refuse to pay income taxes.[16] In short, while speech is not limited to writing and speaking, speech through conduct is subject to scrutiny to determine if the expressive aspect (speech) is not overshadowed by activities that are not contemplated as constituting speech.[17] As the *Rumsfeld* decision made quite clear through the examples cited by the court, virtually any human activity might be construed as speech.

Defining the limits of "free" is not so simple. Yet, it is "freedom of speech" and not "speech" that is protected by "doctrinal law"—consisting of constitutions, statutes, and case law.[18] The distinction between all speech and legally protected speech is critical because no one seriously argues that free speech means the right to say or publish whatever you want about anyone or anything without consequences, though the US First Amendment as sometimes interpreted by a minority of the US Supreme Court has come exceedingly close to such an interpretation. The distinction between speech and protected speech demonstrates why free speech theory is an integral aspect of any analysis of doctrinal law. Free speech theory seeks to define the reasons why certain types of speech should be accorded the special status of free speech. Without sound underlying theory, laws dealing with speech would be difficult to evaluate and could be viewed as arbitrary. It is theory that sets forth the goals and expectations of free speech and some of the major theories routinely relate to specific types of speech that should be accorded free speech status.

US Supreme Court Justice Oliver Wendell Holmes once observed that free speech does not give the right to yell "fire" in a crowded theatre.[19] Similarly, most free speech advocates would not be heard to advocate that a computer hacker should be free to publish missile launch codes that activate nuclear weapons systems or that someone should be free to change speed limit signs on motorways. Yet all of these activities clearly involve speech or expression of some sort. In the context of defamation law, unlimited free speech would give the right to defame or injure someone's reputation with legal impunity. From the viewpoint of privacy, unrestricted speech would allow publication of an individual's bank records or medical history. Under all common law legal systems, there are limitations on the right to defame or invade privacy with impunity. Free speech is therefore the realm of speech that is not limited or restrained by another body of law.

A starting place for free speech is perhaps Article 19 of the *Universal Declaration of Human Rights* (Universal Declaration), adopted by the United Nations General Assembly in 1948 that, in very broad terms, acknowledges that freedom of expression is a basic human right:

> Everyone has the right to freedom of opinion and expression; this right includes freedom to hold opinions without interference and to seek, receive and impart information and ideas through any media regardless of frontiers.

However, having established this universal right in Article 19, then there is the limitation in Article 29 (2):

> In the exercise of his rights and freedoms, everyone shall be subject only to such limitations as are determined by law solely for the purpose of securing due recognition and respect for the rights and freedoms of others and of meeting the just requirements of morality, public order and the general welfare in a democratic society.

Freedom of expression, even if a universal right, is certainly something less than an absolute if it is subject to requirements of respect for the rights and freedoms of others as well as morality and public order. Article 10 of the European Convention for the Protection of Human Rights and Fundamental Freedoms also presents freedom of expression as a right balanced by somewhat vague limitations:

> Everyone has the right to freedom of expression. This right shall include freedom to hold opinions and to receive and impart information and ideas without interference by public authority and regardless of frontiers....
>
> The exercise of these freedoms...may be subject to such formalities, conditions, restrictions or penalties as are prescribed by law and are necessary in a democratic society, in the interests of national security, territorial integrity or public safety, for the prevention of disorder or crime, for the protection of health or morals, for the protection of the reputation or rights of others.

Although not expressed as an exception to Article 10, under Article 8, the European Convention gives privacy equal dignity to freedom of expression: "Everyone has the right to respect for his private and family life, his home and his correspondence." This right is subject to the same type of limitation as the Article 10 rights. Not surprisingly, there is an inherent tension, if not conflict, between Article 8 and 10.[20]

Section 2 of the Canadian Charter of Rights and Freedoms provides that "Everyone has the following fundamental freedoms... (b) freedom of thought, belief, opinion and expression, including freedom of the press and other media of communication." Against this broad grant, Section 1 of the Canadian Charter permits the government to impose reasonable limits.[21] In contrast to both European and Canadian law, the First Amendment of the US Constitution speaks in sweeping and ostensibly unrestricted language:

> Congress shall make no law respecting an establishment of religion, or prohibiting the free exercise thereof; or abridging the freedom of speech, or of the press; or the right of the people peace-

> ably to assemble, and to petition the government for a redress of grievances.

As discussed in chapter 7, the American First Amendment is peculiar because it is not so much a guarantee of freedom of expression as a prohibition of government regulation of speech. In contrast, the Constitution of the state of California is an express, but not unrestricted, grant to the people, more in line with the European Convention and the Canadian Charter, and provides:

> Every person may freely speak, write and publish his or her sentiments on all subjects, being responsible for the abuse of this right. A law may not restrain or abridge liberty of speech or press.[22]

While Article 19 of the Universal Declaration establishes freedom of expression as a basic human right, many of the participating nations were and continue to be totalitarian regimes and consequently, Article 19 is considered as being more of an aspiration than reflecting actual recognition by all of the signatory states. However, Article 19 does not explain why everyone should have the right to "freedom of opinion and expression." While human rights pronouncements state that freedom of expression is essential, they do not persuasively address why these rights are essential. As acknowledged by Article 29 of the Universal Declaration, free speech has always been a limited right. Determining the proper limitation on free speech is still not fully resolved because even within the specific limitation of something as thoroughly hammered out as defamation laws; the balance of interests between freedom of expression and other rights is not static. Questions regarding the legitimate and reasonable limitations on free speech frequently require recourse to the underlying reasons and theories justifying free speech.

For example, while no one would seriously contend that free speech, as a basic human right, entitles a citizen to turn over military secrets to an enemy during wartime as a permissible exercise of free speech, the question becomes far more difficult if free speech rights are curtailed to prevent a citizen from criticising a government's conduct of a war. In this case, the distinction may be that the former involves an action that clearly and immediately risks harm and injury to others while the latter is more properly part of democratic government and does not involve the certainty of injury to other members of society. While the distinctions are frequently difficult, the result is that freedom of speech has always been limited to some extent. Some of the recognised exceptions to guarantees of freedom of speech where there may be extensive government or legal regulation include:

- Child pornography
- Obscenity
- Speech harmful to children
- Radio and television broadcasts
- Defamatory publications
- Government employees' political activities
- Incitement of imminent lawless action
- Time, place, and manner restrictions such as noise limits near hospitals
- Compelled speech such as truth in advertising
- Conspiracy to commit crimes
- Children's free speech in schools
- Speech protected by copyright and trademark
- Private speech not involving government regulation
- Speech endangering national security
- Unauthorised disclosure of personal financial or medical records

With so many exceptions, it is difficult to acknowledge speech as being free except to say that many societies claim to encourage free speech but invariably restrict speech in numerous ways. In the United States, free speech is guaranteed by the First Amendment and the exceptions have to be justifiable in light of the constitutional right. While the First Amendment on its face only applies to government initiated or sponsored interference with speech, it is not always easy to distinguish between private and public activities. This seminal question for any First Amendment analysis promises to become even more challenging as governments increasingly elect to contract public services to private entities. However, the trend has been for increasingly restrictive interpretation of "public" thereby removing matters found to be essentially private from the protection of the First Amendment.

Despite the broad language of the First Amendment, even in the United States, free speech is not always assured even in such bastions of debate and learning as universities. Today, many universities have in place codes of conduct that govern speech with the goal of maintaining a more pleasant learning experience for students. These limitations, even if not recognised by traditional free speech theory, find justification when sociological principles are applied. In jurisdictions where the right to free speech is not expressly guaranteed by a constitution, the laws can be more flexible with the result that free speech may not really be a guaranteed right but exists only as what remains after considering the laws restraining speech. Or, in the case of Germany, free speech is a recognised right but it exists as a right subordinate to the right to dignity, including privacy. In the next chapter, a sociological explanation is articulated to provide an explanation for freedom of speech rights that fluctuate from one society to the other.

Recognising that various laws provide for some level of freedom of expression as well as limits on that freedom, the question remains as to what constitutes the appropriate limits or rather, what type of speech should be free. If the question is posed, "do you desire freedom of speech?" It is difficult to imagine anything other than a strong affirmative response. For hundreds of years, but most particularly in the past one hundred and fifty years, legal philosophers and legal theorists have been compiling specific reasons why freedom of speech is desirable. At one extreme, there is an entire branch of free speech theory, known as the constitutive justification, built around the concept that free speech is desirable because it is good for the well-being of the individual—a scholarly statement meaning free speech is good because "I like it" or "It makes me feel good." While this might appear to be only a visceral response and hardly the material on which legal doctrine is constructed, this reasoning, in fact, very roughly summarises aspects of Immanuel Kant's significant contribution to freedom of speech discourse. With the exception of the First Amendment, all of the major bodies of doctrinal law expressly provide for freedom of speech balanced against some other interests such as defence or public order. Yet, the philosophical theories generally do not recognise these limitations. However, application of sociology theory justifies the countervailing social forces that permit the moderation of otherwise unrestricted freedom of expression.

It seems that all of the free speech theorists have put their own gloss on the subject and further refine and parse out specific reasons and arguments for freedom of speech. Not surprisingly, many of these theories overlap or are simply subsets of existing theories. However, virtually all of the theories can be categorised within a taxonomy used by the American legal philosopher Ronald Dworkin and others that identifies the theories as falling within instrumental or constitutive justifications. The instrumental justification points to specific outcomes that are fostered by types of free expression. This body of theory is most commonly applied to political speech. An example of this is the widely held belief that democratic government is supported by freedom of expression concerning political parties and candidates for elective office. In contrast, the constitutive justification relates to arguments that speech is not desirable to attain a specific end or goal, but rather that freedom of expression is desirable for its own intrinsic value such as enhancing human dignity.

Dworkin actually navigated a rather direct approach toward a sociological description of the constitutive justification but did so without recourse to specific sociological theory:

> First, morally responsible people insist on making up their own minds about what is good or bad in life or in politics, or what is

> true and false in matters of justice or faith. Government insults its citizens, and denies their moral responsibility, when it decrees that they cannot be trusted to hear opinions that might persuade them to dangerous or offensive convictions. We retain our dignity, as individuals, only by insisting that no one, no official and no majority, has the right to withhold an opinion from us on the ground that we are not fit to hear and consider it.
>
> For many people moral responsibility has another, more active, aspect as well: a responsibility not only to form convictions of one's own, but to express these to others, out of respect and concern for them, and out of a compelling desire that truth be known, justice served, and the good secured.[23]

While Dworkin focused on the individual, his arguments are not at odds with the application of sociological theory and are harmonious with concepts espoused by Habermas. Indeed, it is but a short theoretical jump from Dworkin's explanation of the constitutive justification to the argument that all free speech can be justified instrumentally because freedom of expression is essential to the smooth running of society. That is, to accomplish efficient community functions, where society is typified by an extreme division of labour, broad rights of freedom of expression are essential.

In the next chapter, a sociologically based theory will be presented that provides a reason why the constitutive justification is ultimately instrumental because broad, topically unrestricted speech rights for individuals are essential in societies permeated with social as well as economic division of labour. Furthermore, sociology assists in interpreting philosophical theory from the perspective of communal as opposed to merely individual values. This intervention of sociological theory is necessary, or at least helpful, because while almost all of the traditional free speech theories find reasonable acceptance, none are applied without exception and modification and, the theories themselves usually speak in absolutes and do not, on their face, condone the legitimacy of moderation.

ENDNOTES

1. See, for example, Randall Bezanson, *Speech Stories: How Free Can Speech Be?* (discussion of cross-burning, flag burning, pornography, offensive words on clothing and other situations where speech and conduct seem to collide).
2. The communicative and political aspects of art can be extremely important in evaluating whether the art is protected from censorship. See Randall Bezanson, *Art and Freedom of Speech* 7–49 (discussion of Karen Finley performance artist).
3. Ira Robbins, "Digitus Impudicus: The Middle Finger and the Law", *California Davis Law Review* 41 (2008): 1403.
4. 547 US 47 (2006).
5. 10 USCA s 983(b) (Supp.2005).
6. *Forum for Academic and Institutional Rights, Inc v. Rumsfeld,* 291 F Supp 2d 269 (D NJ 2003).
7. *Forum for Academic and Institutional Rights, Inc v. Rumsfeld,* 390 F 3d 219 (3d Cir 2004).
8. See Haig Bosmajian, *The Freedom Not to Speak,* 204.
9. *West Virginia v. Barnette,* 319 US 624 (1943).
10. *Wooley v. Maynard,* 430 US 705 (1977). To meet the objections of pacifists, the state of New Hampshire subsequently offered "Scenic" as an alternative.
11. *United States v. Eichman,* 496 US 310 (1990); *Texas v. Johnson,* 491 US 397 (1989). Both of these cases were decided on 5-4 majorities reflecting the continuing controversy over the legality of flag burning as lawful expressive conduct.
12. *Rumsfeld,* 547 US 47, 66 (2006).
13. Margaret Blanchard, *Revolutionary Sparks—Freedom of Expression in America,* 457–459.
14. See cases discussed in Robert Goldstein, *Flag Burning & Free Speech,* 245–254.
15. The 9-0 vote of the justices can be somewhat deceptive because there is not any justice currently sitting on the Supreme Court who has a reputation for defending symbolic or nonverbal speech but had there been a justice with such a predisposition, the overall vote could have been significantly different and possibly even have reached an opposite conclusion. The late

Justices William O. Douglas and Thurgood Marshall were both strong advocates of protecting symbolic speech. See Haig Bosmajian, *Justice Douglas and Freedom of* Speech, xx.

16. *Rumsfeld,* 547 US 47, 66–67 (2006).
17. Brook Bristow, "King Solomon: Did the Supreme Court Make a Wise Decision in Upholding the Solomon Amendment in Rumsfeld v Forum for Academic & Institutional Rights, Inc.?", *Mercer Law Review* 58 (2007): 815.
18. Frederick Schauer, "The Boundaries of the First Amendment: A Preliminary Exploration of Constitutional Salience", *Harvard Law Review* 117 (2004): 1765, 1769–1774.
19. *Abrams v. US*, 250 US 616 (1919).
20. See Jonathan Coad, "Reynolds and Public Interest–What About Truth and Human Rights?" *Entertainment Law Review* 18, no. 3 (2007): 75.
21. Canadian Charter of Rights and Freedoms, Part 1 of the *Canada Act*, 1982, Schedule B to the *Canada Act 1982* (UK), chapter 11.
22. *California Constitution*, Article I, Section 2(a).
23. Ronald Dworkin, *Freedom's Law—The Moral Reading of the American Constitution*, 200.

Chapter 2

The Sociology of Freedom of Speech

Introduction

Discussions of freedom of speech normally focus on the rights of the individual. However, the benefits of freedom of expression—even under traditional theory—frequently belong as much to society as to the individual, and the benefits flowing to society may indeed be different than the individual rights. For example, in the well-regarded democracy theory propounded by Professor Meiklejohn, the direct benefit of the individuals' right to engage in political discussion is the advancement of democratic government which is clearly a societal benefit. While good government may be of benefit to the individual, the existence of democracy is societal or belongs to the group rather than just an individual. A central feature of Durkheim's approach to sociology is that society is not merely a collection of individuals but is more akin to a living organism constituted of millions of living cells. While the cells possess aspects of life, the organism has a character and existence distinctly unique from its constituent cells. Similarly, society has an existence separate and apart from the individuals occupying the social group, and the social group may be studied as having its own distinct existence. In this discussion, the focus will be on freedom of expression having direct and virtually independent benefit to the social organism as opposed to the real but distinct benefits to the individual members of society.

A distinction or dichotomy between the social approach and the individual approach is that society has separate requirements for it to flourish and be successful than has the individual, and rights designed to focus on promoting and fostering individualism may lead to social ructions or disharmony in society as a whole. The solution is likely to involve a balancing of the different interests as is contemplated by the European Convention that specifically recognises both privacy and freedom of expression as basic rights.

While social science–based studies have been used to demonstrate how people actually engage in speech, this discussion will undertake a more fundamental and less empirical mission.[1] It will pursue an approach based on the pioneering work of Emile Durkheim brought current by the ideas of Jurgen Habermas. Sociology is not being used in the conventional sense, such as a statistical study of behaviour, but rather as a theoretical study of the free speech expectations predicted by the structure of society itself. These free speech expectations should then be memorialised or institutionalised through laws. A sociological perspective of law has been defined as being an analysis or "perspective informed by social theory."[2] This discussion will employ sociological principles to ascertain the free speech expectations of a modern democratic society in which individual roles are marked by a very developed social and economic division of labour. The general thrust of the argument is that free speech and the laws surrounding speech are a function of the type of society being examined. Freedom of speech is an essential component determined by many social factors—most particularly, the division of labour in society.

Among the traditional justifications for free speech, with the exception of the democracy theory (discussed in chapter 5), which states that freedom of speech concerning political matters and elections is necessary for democratic government to function, the other theories speak not so much in terms of group necessity but in terms of how free speech may assist in the furtherance of some individual goal such as self-fulfilment. It is in this context that sociological theory is offered for a coherent validation of an expansive grant of free speech to all of the members of society. The crux of this argument is that expansive free speech rights are essential for the existence and prosperity of a modern industrial state; however, this argument also underscores that the right of expression does not exist in a vacuum and must be balanced with other legitimate expectations of society. Freedom of speech is not simply desirable from a philosophical point of view, but it is essential for the survival of highly industrialised societies. This viewpoint is not at odds with traditional constitutive and instrumental justifications for freedom of speech. In fact, the traditional free speech concepts undoubtedly connect to the sociological explanation, and the sociological argument supports the view that the constitutive justification for freedom of speech is actually instrumental—that is, broad generalised speech rights are essential to the smooth running of complex societies. The connection between sociology and philosophy will in part be found through an expansive interpretation of the free speech theory known as "self-realisation" that contains elements of both instrumental and constitutive justifications for freedom of speech.[3] The sociological explanation offered by Habermas demonstrates how self-realisation is not just desirable from a philosophical point of view but is also required for individuals to effectively and happily function in advanced societies. If the sociological explanation is correct, the prognosis for advanced societies that employ legal systems to restrict freedom of speech unduly may not be so good. Social disintegration may be the ultimate consequence of disconnect between law and society.

As an approach to freedom of speech issues, the sociological explanation presents a number of positive contributions. First, unlike traditional free speech analysis, sociology does not require fine distinctions between instrumental and constitutive justifications. The sociological explanation is, in a sense, an instrumental justification that subsumes individual autonomy arguments found in the constitutive justification. Second, the sociological explanation is, by definition, directly linked to real-world situations and, while perhaps lacking the elegance or clarity of the philosophers' logic, represents freedom of speech as it must exist in modern highly developed societies. Third, the sociological argument presents an opportunity to connect doctrinal law with theory. Fourth, both Weber and Durkheim argued that sociology explains why and how different kinds of societies correlate with different kinds of laws.[4] An essential aspect of the sociological argument centres on the intimate relation between laws and local societal values or norms. For example, while England and the United States are both modern industrial states, they are not identical in terms of history and culture and, consequently, their laws should not be expected to be the same but should be expected to be similar, and this expectation is borne out by reality. Fifth, the sociological explanation accommodates balancing free speech rights with rights to reputation and privacy.

In sum, a sociological explanation may be considered as either an independent basis for freedom of speech or, as the missing link—the Realpolitik that unites philosophy with doctrinal law. Before undertaking a sociological explanation for freedom of speech and because sociological theory is not the traditional language for explaining freedom of speech, it is necessary to become conversant, if not comfortable, with some of the language and theoretical models employed by Durkheim and his more contemporary colleague, Habermas.

SOCIOLOGY AND LAW

Even before sociology was established as a discipline, the groundwork supporting a sociological approach to law was established in the early nineteenth century by the German legal scholar and philosopher, Friedrich Karl von Savigny. In response to legal theorists who supported codification as a natural system of law, Savigny argued that law could not be approached from the perspective of idealised codes and statutes but may only be understood as an expression of beliefs that cannot be separated from the manners, morals, customs, and history of the nation. However, Savigny was not a common law enthusiast. He believed that the discovery of a nation's law was not with the judges but with legal scholars. [5] More recently, Professor Vincenzo Zeno-Zencovich has written that freedom of speech "varies according to both time and space" and is "shaped by the community where it is expressed".[6] Similarly, the expression-related tort of defamation has been termed a "distinctively sociological tort."[7]

Defamation law is particularly suited to a sociological analysis. Defamation is an unusual tort in that the wrongful actions of the perpetrator (speaker or publisher) are directed toward third parties and not the victim. This is an atypical situation because in most legally cognisable activities, the harm is inflicted on the victim directly.[8] For example, while a battery consists of a punch or blow directed to the body of the victim, defamation does not consist of diminishing what the victims think of themselves but rather are injuries to victims caused by the speaker or author making third parties think less of the victims—an injury to reputation in the community and not to character or self-esteem itself. Indeed, a key element of defamation is publication to a third party. The relationship between the individual and how the individual is viewed in the broader community invites a sociological analysis.[9]

The formal relationship between sociology and law is, however, essentially a twentieth-century phenomenon because sociology did not really emerge as a distinct social science until Emile Durkheim and Max Weber effectively carved out the territory of this new discipline in the late nineteenth and early twentieth centuries. From the viewpoint of the legal profession, the value of sociology might be defined as the utilisation of sociological concepts to assist in evaluating and even creating legal policy and doctrinal law. From the perspective of the sociologist, the issue would be somewhat reversed, and law would be considered as a constituent element, like popular culture or government, that falls within the all-encompassing scope of the study of society. The question of whether law is one of the aspects of sociology or whether sociological theory should support legal analysis has been the subject of substantial scholarly attention.[10] The study of the relationship between law and sociology has been termed "the sociological movement in law."[11] This movement was built on two sometimes distinct and sometimes less-than-distinct concepts—sociological jurisprudence and the sociology of law. The central players in sociological jurisprudence were legal scholars such as Roscoe Pound whereas the underlying theory used in the sociology of law was furnished by the pioneering work of Max Weber and Emile Durkheim. Durkheim and Weber chronologically preceded the sociological jurisprudence scholars but in terms of the evolution of the sociological movement in law, Weber and Durkheim became influential only after sociological jurisprudence came to prominence.[12]

Sociological jurisprudence is rather limited in scope because it focuses on the behaviour of the legal system, most particularly the courts, rather than the study of law itself.[13] However, a substantial amount of social research continues to be devoted to analysing the operations of various aspects of the legal system including courts, lawyers, prison systems, and the police. For example, the prestigious journal *Law & Society Review* in the December 2011 edition includes articles entitled "Political Liberalism and Political Embeddedness: Understanding Politics in the Work of Chinese Criminal Defense Lawyers" and "Justices and Legal Clarity: Analyzing the Complexity of U.S. Supreme Court Opinions." In these studies, the operations or efficacy of a legal system or process is analysed using the empirical analytical tools of the sociologist. Based on these studies, improvements to or greater understanding of the actual operations of the legal system can hope to be achieved.

In contrast, in the second half of the twentieth century, classical sociological concepts established by Weber and Durkheim were applied to explain law in the broadest sense. This study became known as the sociology of law.[14] Marx did not play such an influential role because while he was one of the classical social theorists, he did not treat law systematically and never developed an actual theory of law. Although the dominant theoretical resources derived from Durkheim and Weber,[15] the applications of sociology of law continued to rest primarily in the hands of legal scholars—in other words, lawyers have put sociology to work to solve issues that legal theory alone could not satisfactorily resolve. One explanation for the dominance of legal scholarship is the "craft mysticism that surrounds law and thus renders it relatively impenetrable to the sociologist."[16] The discussion in this chapter falls somewhere within the broadest parameters of the sociology of law or the sociological movement in law.

Since its emergence as a distinct social science in the late nineteenth and early twentieth centuries, sociology has yielded many theoretical approaches. Unlike the natural sciences, new sociological theories do not displace the old but the theories may coexist. Emile Durkheim (1858–1917) was selected as the sociological theorist to inform this discussion of free speech because unlike many other theorists, Durkheim presents comprehensive or self-contained explanations and rarely leaves open questions. In other words, he squares his theoretical corners and is not fuzzy around the edges. In popular parlance, Durkheim was a bit of a know-it-all. Since the intention is to use sociology to assist in enlightening legal and philosophical issues, theoretical models that leave open questions, even if more fascinating to contemporary sociologists, detract from the essential issue. Furthermore, and not to be overlooked, "Durkheim's writing is direct, concise, and comprehensible."[17] Using a metaphor from physical science, Durkheim presented an approach which has broad application but perhaps does not answer all questions under extreme conditions; just as Newtonian physics fails as velocities approach the speed of light. To resolve all possibilities, sociology may require the complexity of more contemporary theorists like Talcott Parsons or Jurgen Habermas just as physics at the speed of light calls upon Albert Einstein.

Unlike Weber, Durkheim was not a lawyer. Furthermore, Durkheim did not treat law systematically in a single work but, unlike Karl Marx,

Durkheim did not see law as an evil or coercive force used to repress but rather did not harbour any unfriendly beliefs toward laws in general. In fact, especially in his earlier writings, Durkheim frequently addressed legal topics and even suggested that laws constituted essentially verifiable, hard data that could be used to test and measure aspects of society that eluded measurement. At one extreme and perhaps somewhat naively, he even suggested that the sheer volume of laws could be measured as a device to solve sociological questions. Durkheim believed that laws constituted the institutionalisation of societal norms and consequently reflected the values of society.[18] Durkheim recognised that there could be situations where the law was not keeping up with changing societal values, but he believed that ultimately this situation would be rectified or societal cohesion would be adversely affected. He presented, as a key element of his theory for the evolution of society, the belief that laws were sufficiently representative of societal values that laws could be used to measure otherwise ephemeral or ambiguous changes in community values. Simply put, Durkheim comfortably equates law with social control that is derived from society itself; and although he wrote more than a century ago, he remains a standard authority or point of reference for the connection between law and sociology.[19] Ultimately, Durkheim is recognised as the founder of modern sociology[20] because he "gave the science of sociology its status as a legitimate, autonomous and respected university discipline."[21]

THE WORLD ACCORDING TO DURKHEIM

At the time Durkheim first published *The Division of Labor in Society* in 1893, it was still unclear whether sociology was indeed a separate discipline from psychology.[22] One of Durkheim's major contributions and perhaps his most controversial argument and primary divergence from Weber was that society could not be understood by studying the individuals comprising the group but rather that society was, in effect, a distinct living organism, that in turn, defined the characteristics of its members. Through this argument, he attempted to carve out an intellectual niche for sociology that did not fall within any existing and recognised social science. To further this goal, Durkheim developed a comprehensive sociological discipline and created terms of art that he hoped would amount to a scientific lexicon of sociology to enhance his subject as a science. The late nineteenth century and early twentieth century saw an efflorescence of new discoveries in the natural and physical sciences. This was especially true in physics where the largely intuitive and linear world of Newtonian physics was being subjected to new theoretical models culminating in Planck's quantum theory that appeared in 1901 and Einstein's revolutionary ideas including the special theory of relativity which was published in 1905. Durkheim sincerely desired sociology to take its rightful place as a discipline no less serious than physics. He built many of his arguments around an analogy to the human body and argued that just as human beings cannot be fully understood as merely being collections of organs and tissues, similarly, society existed separate and apart from the individuals who were the constituent members of the social group. Durkheim is sometimes viewed as being somewhat conservative but this conservatism perhaps only confirms his insistence that sociology be treated as a serious science and that every argument be subjected to statistical or ethnographic proof.

Durkheim was singularly unimpressed with his predecessor Marx and concluded that Marx's dogma of economic materialism was seriously deficient and reflected basic misunderstandings of social life. In further contrast to Marx, Durkheim had a relatively low opinion of politics and he believed that academics should avoid political involvement. [23] In contrast to Marx, Durkheim believed that religion, as opposed to economics, was the most basic social phenomenon and that everything in society such as law, morality, politics, and science can be traced back to religion. Durkheim argued that economics was not the source of these societal traits but that economics was in fact a circumstance derived from religion.[24] This argument was developed by Max Weber and perhaps reaches its zenith in Weber's text, *The Protestant Ethic and the Spirit of Capitalism* published in 1905 and 1906. In this work, Weber argued that protestant

Christianity was the driving force behind the growth of modern capitalism. Weber specifically ties the growth of capitalism to the theological works of John Calvin (1509-1564).[25]

A still-nascent argument validating Durkheim's rejection of Marxist thought is contained in chapter 4 in which the role of religion in the emergence of urban society is contrasted with the traditional theory that economic factors led to urbanisation and civilisation. Durkheim ultimately concluded that the secondary influence of economics on society required the conclusion that the growth of large-scale capitalist enterprises did not require the overthrow of the existing social order and that Marxist theory was simply factually incorrect and theoretically unsound.[26]

Durkheim viewed humans as creatures defined by the society in which they lived. He viewed human autonomy or free will as being derived from life in a modern complex society in which there was substantial division of labour. He saw society evolving from primitive to complex forms with division of labour as the driving force in this development. Durkheim's concept of division of labour should not be confused with the economic terminology utilised by the classical economists Adam Smith and David Ricardo with respect to the separation of labour functions to improve industrial production. Durkheim conceived of a much broader, sociological concept which he termed the social division of labour. Division of labour encompassed all separations of function among members of society and was not limited to only industrial workers involved in mass production of manufactured goods. From a sociological viewpoint, division of labour attached to every situation in which members of a society did not pursue precisely the same activities. The social division of labour even includes the differentiation among sexual functions between men and women. Durkheim suggests, however, that in the most basic societies, the actual social division of labour between men and women was quite small. Durkheim even goes so far to argue that the institution of marriage itself is a result of the social division of labour between men and women.[27] Durkheim saw a never-ending division of labour as society grew more urbanised and more complex. For example, this included school teachers as being distinct from parents, school principals separate from teachers, and math teachers separate from chemistry teachers.

To Durkheim, social division of labour was the key factor in determining the unifying factor or solidarity of society and, solidarity was a central concept to Durkheim and remained so throughout his writings. Imagine the most basic society of hunter-gatherers where each individual fulfils the same role with no distinctions among their roles. In Durkheim's terminology, these less complex societies were held together by mechanical solidarity where the social facts (that is, roughly, morals) were universally held by all members of the society in their collective conscience because the members performed functions indistinguishable from one another and division of labour was at a minimum. In societies where mechanical solidarity prevailed, any behavioural deviation by a member of the group was an affront to the entire group because all values were shared. As societies evolved through urbanisation and population growth, division of labour allowed for specialisation and the bonds of society were no longer merely mechanical and based on identity of interests but transitioned to what he called organic solidarity—a binding together caused by the dependency of each member to the other. As shared values diminished as a result of division of labour, members of complex societies developed individualism. Extrapolating to a free speech perspective, freedom of expression was both unknown and unnecessary in a society dominated by mechanical solidarity because everyone shared the same beliefs and knowledge—there was very little to talk about, and controversy or conflict would have been minimal.

In the legal manifestation of mechanical versus organic solidarity, Durkheim espoused as one of his fundamental concepts the progression from criminal punishment to civil sanctions or restitution for the same conduct as societies became more complex. He saw this as a function of the division of labour in more complex social settings. In more primitive societies, there was less division of labour among individuals and there was more of a collective conscience which created the mechanical solidarity among members of the group. Since everyone was engaged in the same activities, there existed completely shared values and beliefs. An action which disturbed this collective conscience would amount to a negation of the solidarity of the community conscience. As simply and eloquently stated by Durkheim, the penalty for violating this collective conscience would be penal or repressive:[28]

> [A]n act is criminal when it offends the strong, well-defined states of the collective consciousness.[29]

In other words, we should not say that an act offends the common consciousness because it is criminal, but that it is criminal because it offends that consciousness. We do not condemn it because it is a crime, but it is a crime because we condemn it.[30]

> [P]unishment constitutes an emotional reaction. This characteristic is all the more apparent the less cultured societies are. Indeed primitive peoples punish for the sake of punishing, causing the guilty person to suffer solely for the sake of suffering and without expecting any advantage for themselves from the suffering they inflict upon him.[31]
>
> As for the social character of this reaction, it comes from the social nature of the sentiments offended. Because these are to be found in every individual consciousness the wrong done arouses among all who witness it or who know of its existence the same indignation. All are affected by it; consequently, everybody stiffens himself against the attack. Not only is reaction general, but it is collective, which is not the same thing.... It is public anger. [32]

Organic solidarity exists in more advanced societies with a more defined division of labour with fewer shared values. The collective conscience is largely replaced by a series or collection of differentiated consciences among defined groups within the society.[33] As societies evolve and division of labour increases, the society itself moves from the mechanical to the organic. No longer is a transgression automatically an injury to the public order or the King's Peace. Rather the disturbance or injury may be quite private and not shared by other members of the community. As this societal evolution occurs, Durkheim regarded the law as providing restitution, the traditional civil remedy, to the injured individual rather than imposing a societal punishment on the offender:

> The distinguishing mark of this sanction is that [it]… comes down to a mere restoration of the *status quo ante*. Suffering in proportion to the offence is not inflicted upon the one who has broken the law…. Damages awarded have no penal character: they are simply a means of putting back the clock so as to restore the past, so far as possible, to its normal state. [34]

In terms of human relations, repressive or criminal sanctions are imposed by society itself but restitutionary or civil sanctions are between the individuals directly involved in the circumstances or event:

> Since the rules where sanctions are restitutory do not involve the common consciousness, the relationships that they determine are not of the sort that affect everyone indiscriminately. This means that they are instituted directly, not between the individual and society, but between limited and particular elements in society, which they link to one another.[35]

Although restitution involves individuals rather than an individual interacting with society as a whole, Durkheim recognises that there is a societal role in restitutive sanctions. Society, acting through the state (courts and law making bodies), acts as the intermediary between the individuals.[36]

As originally presented in the *Division of Labor*, all repressive laws would be expected to disappear as the division of social labour in society increased. Of course this does not occur, and in his subsequent works, Durkheim never again raised such an extreme argument. In his later works, he came to recognise that some level of collective conscience would continue to survive even among members of a complex society and therefore, repressive sanctions were still required in situations that continued to affront the collective conscience. He predicted that as the collective conscience diminished with the progression of the division of labour, many acts formerly treated as criminal would become essentially private matters that could be more properly treated as civil disputes susceptible of restitutive sanctions.[37] Historically, various situations come and go from the collective conscience and the criminal law is therefore in a constant state of flux.

The concept of law fits into Durkheim's conception of social solidarity because he postulated that the social facts or morals which define the distinction between complex and more basic societies were difficult to meaningfully catalogue. To Durkheim, law was a measurable and visible index that reflected solidarity within a society. Law provided a solid measuring tool, much like a natural scientist's tools of experimental observation, to facilitate otherwise difficult to quantify societal characteristics.[38] Unlike indistinct moral values, laws were easily discernible and were clearly articulated in the statutes and judicial decisions. Laws, in effect, served as the precise indicators or markers of social facts (morals and values) within society and functioned as "social data."[39] Durkheim believed that legal data would offer scientific proof of how the division of labour resulted in societal transitions from mechanical to organic solidarity. He theorised that mechanical solidarity was typified by repressive (penal) laws whereas organic solidarity would be reflected in a body of laws that is more properly characterised as restitutive, restoring individuals to their prior status before the wrong occurred. Durkheim also attempted to employ empirical evidence of the movement from repressive to restitutive law as proof of the ineluctable movement of advancing societies from the mechanical to the organic. The validity of this theory is discussed in the following chapter where the migration of defamation as a criminal offence to a purely civil tort is discussed.

Mid-Century Criticism of Durkheim and His Theory of Law

Emile Durkheim's "forceful presence"[40] so dominated the emerging discipline of sociology during his own lifetime that it is not surprising that his work eventually attracted substantial criticism by the next generation of sociologists. Durkheim was so determined to define clearly the parameters of sociology that he undoubtedly appeared or did in fact perform as an autocrat protecting his turf from intrusion by economists, psychologists or other social scientists whose contributions might blur the lines between sociology and other disciplines. Habermas actually provides a good example of the consequences of Durkheim's concern of mixing disciplines as the former's thinking is a blend of philosophy, political science, and general unspecified social theory. In addition to the substantial number of books and articles that Durkheim wrote expressing his own views, he also exercised control, at least over French sociology, by editing the annual journal of sociology, *L'Annee Sociologique,* for many years. In this journal, Durkheim and his students prepared many reviews of books authored by other social scientists. Consequently, this gave Durkheim a unique opportunity to critique the work of his contemporaries.[41]

While the statistical approach that Durkheim pioneered clearly has influenced modern sociology and perhaps even defines it as a social science, the data relied on by him was not only quirky and quaint but sometimes incorrect. Durkheim was writing at the beginning of the twentieth century, and the science of the day recognised measuring techniques such as cranial capacity and facial features as constituting sound scientific knowledge. Furthermore, ethnographic data was frequently not much better than anecdotal travelogues lacking in scientific method. When this type of data is coupled with Durkheim's prolonged metaphors to the human body as representing society as distinct from human organs and cells within the organs, it is not difficult to see why some of Durkheim's writing presents challenges for modern readers. Although his theoretical concepts are invariably quite clear, the questionable supporting data sometimes detracts from his arguments. As a result, his original texts may be somewhat cumbersome with the result that far too much reliance has been placed on subsequent explanations and paraphrases of his work. Interpretations and, in some cases, misinterpretations, by later writers may have diminished the contemporary relevance of much of Durkheim's work. The salient exception to this generalisation is Durkheim's groundbreaking study of suicide, which remains the single most important text on the subject .[42]

Nevertheless, despite developments over the past century, Durkheim, like other early sociologists, continues to represent valid sociological theory. Unlike sciences such as chemistry or physics where theories are replaced as new discoveries are made, sociology is not susceptible to such settled principles. Sociology is more of an argumentative discipline, and new sociological theories do not so much replace earlier theories but are more likely to add to the discourse by building on or coexisting with their progenitors.[43] While an overall reevaluation of Durkheim's contributions to sociology is an ongoing exercise,[44] the scope of the evaluation of modern criticism in this discussion shall be limited to the matters relied on concerning solidarity and law. Despite the criticisms, in the context of sociology and the law, Durkheim remains an essential contributor and an important theorist even in the twenty-first century.[45]

While Durkheim utilised the law as a tool in many of his works, he never composed a systematic or unitary treatment of law. However the core concepts are contained in his first work, *The Division of Labor in Society,* in which he proposed three hypotheses about law:[46]

1. Law should be utilised as an external index to measure the nature of social solidarity, whether mechanical or organic.
2. Law evolves as society moves from all-encompassing religiosity to modern secularism, from primitive to complex society, and from collectivism to individualism. The overall shift with the continued complexity of society and division of labour is reflected by the

transition from predominantly repressive or penal law to a system focusing on restitution among individuals.

3. Crime is a violation of the common conscience of society and that punishment for criminal activity has as its real function the maintenance of societal cohesiveness by sustaining the common consciousness.[47]

The discussion in the next chapter of the transition from a combination of criminal and civil defamation to sole reliance on civil defamation is directly relevant to the second of these concepts while the first involves methodology and the third deals, on a more philosophical basis, with the underlying basis for criminal punishment. It is the third point that has attracted most of the serious critical debate among legal scholars. While the second point has attracted critical comment from sociologists, it has not drawn significant attention within the legal community. The first point has been the subject of questioning and even puzzlement by both lawyers and sociologists.

From a legal perspective, perhaps the most interesting challenge to these hypotheses arose in a debate between two eminent twentieth-century legal scholars, Lord Patrick Devlin and H.L.A. Hart. This debate focused on Durkheim's third point which attempts to explain the rationale for criminal punishment. The argument grew around a concept that is known as the "disintegration thesis." In 1958, Lord Devlin began the debate with controversial statements concerning the purpose of criminal law. He maintained that criminal punishments that reflected the public temperament were essential as a cohesive force in society. For example, he took the extreme position that if homosexuality was viewed by society as seriously offensive, then society should have the right to treat the matter as a crime with the goal of seeking its ultimate eradication or else risk the survival of society.[48] Devlin argued that criminal punishment enforcing public attitudes was an essential, coherent force, preventing the disintegration of society.[49]

H.L.A. Hart took issue with Lord Devlin and, relying on an essay by Ronald Dworkin, suggested that empirical evidence did not support the disintegration thesis but that its supporters would be better advised to pursue what was termed the "conservative thesis" which is predicated on the belief that the majority's moral environment is something of value that should be preserved—something clearly less than predicting disintegration of society.[50] In Hart's terms, Devlin was saying that the rightness or wrongness of societal morality was irrelevant but that it was critical that society enforce its prevailing morality or society itself would disintegrate—thus, the disintegration thesis. Hart questioned whether the failure to convert popular prejudices into criminal law would jeopardise the fabric of society [51] and argued that, in the absence of convincing empirical evidence, the conservative thesis was preferable to the more extreme disintegration thesis.[52] On the other end of the philosophical spectrum was the "classical thesis" that maintained that society should be the instrument of a truly moral life based on concepts such as natural justice and fairness as opposed to enforcement of popular prejudices through the criminal law.[53] The classical thesis exalts the role of morality and posits that law should be used to promote an idealised morality. Roots for this vision can be found in the works of Plato and Aristotle.

Professor Hart acknowledged that Lord Devlin's views found support in contemporary sociological theory, and specific reference was made to the work of Talcott Parsons, a prominent American sociologist in the mid-twentieth century. It should be noted that Talcott Parsons is not usually associated with Durkheim because Parsons believed that society consisted of three components: individuals, relationships among individuals, and culture in general. Durkheim consistently maintained that society was separate from individuals and was an entity unto itself that, in turn, influenced how individual members of that society behaved. Despite the distinctions between Durkheim and Parsons, Hart went on to state that examination of the rather complex—some might say impenetrable—work of Parsons was unnecessary because the same point was made by Durkheim in *The Division of Labor* in language that was "relatively clear and briefly expressed" and deals specifically with the enforcement of morality via criminal law.[54]

After implying that Lord Devlin's argument was in some way a rehash of what Durkheim had written as his doctoral thesis in the nineteenth Century, Hart summarised the connection between Durkheim and Devlin by this comparison:

> For Lord Devlin punishment protects the existing morality by repressing or diminishing the number of immoral actions which in themselves are considered to threaten or weaken the common morality. For Durkheim, however, punishment sustains the common morality, not mainly by repressing the immoral conduct, but principally by giving satisfactory vent to a sense of outrage because if the vent were closed the common conscience would lose its energy and the cohesive morality would weaken.[55]

Durkheim and Devlin were arguing that societal cohesion requires a connection between criminal punishment and common morality. Throughout his writings, Durkheim was not only "unashamedly moralistic" but maintained that morality was a sociological concept consisting of popularly shared beliefs in specific historical settings. For Durkheim, life reflected popular morality rather than moral absolutes of high philosophical principles.[56] But there was a subtle difference in the outlooks of Devlin and Durkheim. Devlin believed that repression of what the public considered to be immoral was necessary to sustain a cohesive society and that punishment would repress the offending conduct. Durkheim, however, was arguing a related but different point—that the key factor was not the use of punishment to repress immoral conduct but rather that social cohesion required that the conscience collective be vindicated and that this vindication was achieved through punishment of transgressors. Devlin was focusing on punishing the offender to repress antisocial conduct whereas Durkheim was arguing that overall social cohesion was sustained by punishing deviation from popular morality.

In response to Devlin, Hart argued that elected leaders in a democracy had an affirmative duty to enact laws that reflected justice and that there were limits to imposition of majoritarian will.[57] Durkheim was not expressing any moral judgment and might not necessarily object to Hart's argument but would have added that if the legislators failed to convince the population of the merit of taking the higher moral road, the laws would indeed fail to reflect the conscience collective and would not support societal cohesion. From a political standpoint, if elected leadership continually enacts laws that are not harmonious with community values, the citizens will ultimately elect more responsive leaders. Devlin, in contrast, was taking the more extreme position that morality is simply a matter of popular opinion and that the law should reflect this morality or societal disintegration is the inevitable result.

While Durkheim supports Devlin's arguments that societal coherence requires laws that reflect societal values, Durkheim was not disputing or even addressing the core of Hart's arguments that lawmakers have an affirmative duty to be just and to persuade the electorate to be just. Rather, Durkheim was warning that if laws and the collective conscience remained in a disharmonious relationship, then societal cohesion would suffer. In this respect, Durkheim was restating Savigny's argument that law could not be an abstract ideal and had to reflect popular belief and culture. However, this did not directly contradict the argument that legislators had a duty to educate citizens to accept new and more-enlightened concepts. *The Federalist Papers* authored by Alexander Hamilton, John Jay, and James Madison which advocated to the people of New York the ratification of the US Constitution are a clear example of just such a polemic addressed by civic leaders to an unconvinced public.[58]

Hart also attempted to refute Devlin by engaging in some logical legerdemain. Hart indicted Devlin by attacking Durkheim in connection with an ostensible flaw in *The Division of Labor* that is singularly irrelevant because it was neither relied upon by Lord Devlin nor was it germane to the issues being debated between Hart and Devlin. Specifically, Hart attacked Durkheim's first legal hypothesis that law can be used as a quantitative measuring device for otherwise unquantifiable social facts or morals. Hart questioned the use of law as a measuring tool for quantifying mechanical and organic solidarity:

> Somewhat fantastically Durkheim thinks that the law can be used as a measuring instrument. We have merely to count the number of rules which at any time constitute the criminal law and the number of rules which constitute the civil law expressing the division of labour, and then we know what fraction to assign to the relative importance of the two forms of solidarity.[59]

This criticism raised by Hart has had an unfortunate consequence among some legal scholars. The concept of just weighing up the criminal and civil laws reflects, from the viewpoint of lawyers and legal scholars, a very naïve approach that fails to consider the practical problems inherent in trying to decipher whether laws are repressive or restitutionary and how to physically conduct the tabulation.[60] Indeed, sociologists have also complained that Durkheim's use of law as a quantitative device is a "superficially straightforward exercise" that contains "endless methodological problems."[61] However, recourse to Durkheim's actual language in another section of *The Division of Labor*, used in a slightly different context, makes it clear that Durkheim recognised that quantitative measurement was at best an approximation. Durkheim's actual words demonstrate that Hart's criticism is largely misplaced because Durkheim came to recognise that laws were not susceptible to precise calculation as if the issue involved the counting of beans:

> [W]e need, not to count the number of rules, but to group them into classes and sub-classes, depending on whether they relate to the same sentiment or to different ones, or to different varieties of the same sentiment.... *Very clearly such a classification cannot be very complete, nor perfectly rigorous.* Yet for the conclusions we are seeking to draw [classification and listing of crimes], it is more than sufficient and precise.[62] (emphasis added)

Durkheim's actual words so clearly refute Hart's objection that it is as if Hart relied upon an inaccurate interpretation of *The Division of Labor*.[63] Furthermore, Durkheim did not persist in this first hypothesis and it does not appear in his later works.

Moving beyond the Hart-Devlin debate on social cohesion and disintegration, Durkheim's hypothesis that laws moved from repressive to restitutive as society moved from the primitive to the complex through the increase in division of labour has received very little attention from the legal community. However, among sociologists, serious arguments and substantial evidence have accumulated, indicating that Durkheim was factually incorrect in postulating that mechanical solidarity in less complex societies would turn every offence into a matter for repressive and frequently brutal punishment. A number of studies show that so-called primitive societies frequently feature restitutionary as opposed to repressive sanctions. However, this criticism is overstated for at least two reasons. First, and most important, Durkheim, at the theoretical level, was dealing with idealised types of societies. All societies present aspects of both mechanical and organic solidarity to various degrees and Durkheim was addressing evolutionary trends and movement.[64] Second, the ethnographic studies cited by Durkheim have sometimes proven to be flawed and these empirical deficiencies have been unjustifiably used to indict the underlying theory.[65]

To empirically validate his theories, Durkheim relied on patchy ethnographic information concerning Australian Aborigines and Pacific Islanders that was frequently incorrect. Contemporary studies have established that the history of these groups does not support the concept of brutal repressive sanctions existing as a matter of course in less complex societies.[66] However, the real error may have been Durkheim's selection of modern preindustrial societies as evidence of societal evolution in modern industrial states. These small, isolated groups did not develop the substantial social divisions of labour found in modern Europe and North America. To try to understand modern European evolution by looking at smaller, less complex societies that still exist in the modern world raises serious methodological questions and is difficult to justify.

Since contemporary, less complex societies did not evolve into complex societies, it appears anomalous to test a theory of societal evolution using societies that have never undergone evolution, namely, the development of substantial division of labour. In fact, Durkheim is quite clear that evolution from mechanical to organic solidarity cannot take place without a corresponding increase in what he termed dynamic or moral density. The division of labour was contingent on increases in this moral density which basically refers to large populations living in close proximity:[67]

> The division of labour varies in direct proportion to the volume and density of societies and if it progresses in a continuous manner over the course of social development it is because societies become regularly more dense and generally more voluminous.[68]

Durkheim was theorising societal evolution—evolution that was directly contingent on people living in close proximity, that is, urbanisation. While cultures that have never developed cities are certainly interesting and no less virtuous than urbanised cultures, there are nevertheless significant differences between cultures that have urbanised and those that have not. If the concepts of mechanical and organic solidarity are examined in the context of societies that have undergone urbanisation, the validity of Durkheim's theoretical model is enhanced and more relevant to actual events.[69] While a thoroughly researched study of changes in American or English society is beyond the parameters of this present effort, simple recourse to US legal history, even apart from specific laws relating to freedom of speech such as defamation law, lends support to the transition of sanctions from repressive to restitutive as social solidarity moves from the mechanical to the organic.

European colonisation of North America only has a four-hundred-year history, and the period of development of complex division of labour is even briefer. America's urbanisation and industrial development occurred later than in Europe and covers less than two hundred years. Even during the past fifty years as society achieved greater complexity, Americans have witnessed the decline of offences for which capital punishment may be imposed. Furthermore, the wildly repressive laws of the Massachusetts Bay Colony stand in stark contrast to the socially liberal policies of the contemporary Commonwealth of Massachusetts.[70] In England, capital punishment, once a standard remedy for felonies, has been abolished. However, the growth of civil restitutive law has not known any bounds, and new areas of restitutionary law have developed, such as antitrust law, securities regulation law, consumer warranty law, and environmental law where companies or individuals may be required to restore (restitution) the physical or economic landscape that industry or agriculture has despoiled.

Of course, criminal law still exists in modern industrial societies. Durkheim hypothesised that criminal law existed because it was part of the collective conscience of a society. As long as there remain some matters in the collective conscience of the majority, there will be criminal laws. Furthermore, the conscience collective is not static and is constantly changing within a society. Marital infidelity was once punishable by severe criminal sanctions, and divorce required proof of severe misbehaviour. Today, in the United States and England for example, marital relations are completely within the realm of civil law with the exception of physical violence. When a marriage is dissolved, civil law requires an equitable division of marital community assets without recrimination.

The growth of information technology may also affect the relationship between criminal and civil law. With information passing virtually instantaneously among nations, a nation's conscience collective may very well become less localised as it reflects customs and morals from other parts of the world. This instantaneous sharing of information may lead to more uniformity in public morals or the conscience collective with the result that laws become more uniform among nation states. Furthermore, activities that once did not seriously offend the conscience collective, like drinking alcohol while operating automobiles, may transition into activities requiring seriously repressive punishments such as lengthy imprisonment rather than mere fines and suspension of driving privileges. In sum, while not perfect, Durkheim's fundamental concepts of mechanical and organic solidarity still find validity despite a century of criticism and scrutiny.

Organic Solidarity, the Rise of Freedom of Speech, and the Influence of Jurgen Habermas

While Durkheim emphasised the transition from penal to restitutionary law, the same thinking also provides a new way of considering the role of free speech in society. Just as he theorised the evolution of law from penal to restitutive, Durkheim also contemplated the evolution of social change with respect to individual rights. Durkheim argued that as the division of labour increases and society becomes more specialised, individual members of a society acquire greater autonomy and acquire wider personal rights in proportion to the complexity of society:

> But the further one travels in history, the more one is aware of the process of change. In the early stage, the individual personality is lost in the depths of the social mass, and then later, by its own effort, breaks away. From being limited and of small regard, the scope of the individual life expands and becomes the exalted object of moral respect. The individual comes to acquire ever wider rights over his own person and over the possessions to which he has title; he also comes to form ideas about the world that seem to him most fitting and to develop his essential qualities without hindrance.[71]

While the collective conscience dominates in less complex society, Durkheim recognised that with the ever more specialised division of labour attendant in more complex society, the individual acquires a greater appreciation of self or individuality and with that grows the individual's desire to "freely develop his essential qualities without hindrance." Since speech is biologically a human characteristic, it is indeed part of human nature to communicate. As the members of society develop their own nature, this would include their actions which necessarily encompass expressive activity. To develop these qualities without hindrance recognises that speech must be unhindered, that is, free. This conclusion requires further examination.

Durkheim maintained that democracy was the system of government most appropriate to organic solidarity and "that conforms best to our present day notion of the individual."[72] It is also essential to recognise that Durkheim believed that government or the state had a crucial role to play in the advancement of society and that totalitarian societies perverted the progressions that he predicted as society moved from mechanical solidarity to organic solidarity. For example, punishment instead of moving from repressive to restitutionary as the division of labour increased might instead become even more repressive in the event of an authoritarian government.[73] He maintained that democracy had a moral superiority to other forms of government because it was not based on passive obedience or submission but on reflection and communication between the citizen and the government.[74] Durkheim's logic is that advanced societies are marked by a highly developed division of labour which in turn, or correspondingly, results in organic solidarity and, almost by definition, creates an enhanced state of individual autonomy because activities and perceptions are no longer uniform across the population. As discussed in chapter 5, legal philosophers have taken on board the concept of human autonomy as a constitutive justification for freedom of speech. In addition, the most appropriate form of government for such a society is democracy which requires a constant exchange of communications among its members. In other words, organic solidarity, which represents advanced societies, requires or indeed results in enhanced freedom of communication for the individual. That is, freedom of expression is necessitated by organic solidarity itself.

It is important that the freedom to communicate necessitated by organic solidarity is not limited to matters only relating to government but rather extends to all aspects of social life. In the idealised primitive society where mechanical solidarity prevails, everyone is engaged in the same activity as hunter-gatherers and all beliefs and activities are commonly shared; there are no negotiations among individuals and the world view is uniform. In the world of organic solidarity, each individual performs a different task or function. For society to work in this environment, a great deal of coordination is necessary. The amount of coordination involved in simply getting food from growers to supermarket is intricate and constantly self-correcting as orders are placed, prices are negotiated, shippers are contracted, sales clerks are hired, prices are set and advertised, and goods are sold. None of this happens automatically; it requires coordination among all of the participating individuals and this coordination is achieved through agreement among the constituent members of what each shall do and the terms of their performance. To achieve this agreement, there is only one mechanism—communication in all its forms.

Durkheim sociologically presents a case for freedom of expression based on the social division of labour. As mechanical solidarity or group conscience diminishes, the concept of self advances and the individual comes to form personal ideas. In other words, the division of labour creates a situation where individualised communication without governmental hindrance is essential. In a totalitarian political environment, such as the People's Republic of China, communication concerning political matters is highly restricted. But, in the economic sphere where free markets rule, speech is relatively unrestricted because this is necessary.

These conclusions find continuing validity in the work of contemporary social philosopher Jurgen Habermas who has written extensively on the structure of modern society. Like Durkheim, Habermas has been a prolific writer and it is quite impossible to summarise his thinking which has been far ranging and exceedingly complex. For purposes of this discussion, reliance will frequently be made to an excellent and concise summary of his work that was prepared by James Gordon Finlayson and aptly titled *Habermas, A Very Short Introduction.*[75] Born in 1929, Habermas studied in Germany and experienced many transformations in German society—

he was a teenager in the final years of the Third Reich, a young adult in Cold War West Germany, and a mature observer of German reunification and the emergence of the European Union. Throughout these times, he has been a prodigious writer and his thinking, clearly multidisciplinary, has been extremely influential among his peers in Europe. Initially heavily influenced by Marx, with maturity, Habermas has become an ardent exponent of liberal democracy and strong influences of Durkheim, Max Weber, and Talcott Parsons can be found in his work.

Like Durkheim, and unlike legal theorists such as Ronald Dworkin or Frederick Schauer, Habermas does not directly address freedom of expression in a discrete theoretical argument but rather through his conceptualisation of liberal democratic society, which nonetheless makes a rather convincing case for the necessity of freedom of expression. While far more complex than Durkheim's view of modern society as explained through division of labour and organic solidarity, Habermas's societal construct also requires freedom of expression for effective operation. Central to this conclusion are Habermas's theories of discourse ethics and communicative action. Before even venturing a modest summary of some of Habermas's theory, it is essential to acknowledge the complexity, if not convolution, of his work. For example, his *Theory of Communicative Action* (1981) is contained in two volumes and exceeds 1100 pages in the English version. His other works are short only by comparison.

Habermas can be viewed at different levels or altitudes. From a high earth orbit, Habermas does not takes sides between Weber and Durkheim but sees the world as consisting of both Max Weber's concept of society as a collection of individuals and Durkheim's concept of society as a unique organism separate and apart from its constituent members. However, Habermas marks a clear departure from the classical sociologists with his very contemporary concept that society consists of both *lifeworld* and *system*. In Habermas's universe, the members of a society have a different perspective than an observer exterior to that society. From the point of view of the individual members of society, there exists only the lifeworld and from the observer's perspective, there also exists a *system* which is largely invisible to members of the lifeworld.[76] *Life-world* is the world of social life including family, friends, neighbours and voluntary associations. Communication is the medium of the lifeworld.[77] *System*, on the other hand, is an external force embedded into and channelling the lifeworld. By *system*, Habermas is referring to forces such as capitalist economy and political structures that guide the behaviour of members of the lifeworld.[78] The lifeworld is self-standing as it consists of people relating with each other while *system* can only exist to the extent it is embedded within the lifeworld. While lifeworld operates through consensus, systems impose external constraints on the behaviour of life-world participants. Habermas sees a tension between lifeworld and system in which the latter is constantly intruding on the former. In his view, life-world, built on communication and consensus among members of society, is always subject to disharmony or "social pathologies" caused by intrusion of system which can modify behaviour of citizens.[79]

Habermas suggests that in primitive societies, lifeworld and system are closely integrated and that as society evolves into more complex forms, lifeworld and system diverge and exist as opposing elements.[80] While this transition is reasonably consistent with Durkheim's view of the transition from mechanical to organic solidarity, this is not to equate lifeworld and system to mechanical and organic solidarity. They are distinctly different concepts. In more primitive societies, mechanical solidarity exists by virtue of the uniformity of both physical activity and social beliefs of the members of the social group. In such a society, there is minimal distinction among individual members. As the division of labour increases with the advancement of social structures, the unity of mechanical solidarity gives way to the more individualistic or autonomous world of organic solidarity in which members of the social system no longer share common functions and viewpoints but, through their interactions, comprise a new type of social unity—organic solidarity. To Habermas, there is a similar evolution. The unity of lifeworld and system diverge as society evolves to the point where the lifeworld of the citizens is something apart from the embedded system that operates as an external constraint on members of the lifeworld.[81] In more primitive societies where mechanical solidarity prevails and all values are shared, system or power structure is uniform with lifeworld.

Habermas and Durkheim also share a rather similar view of law in society. Durkheim's third hypothesis was that criminal law maintains the conscience collective by sustaining the common conscience.[82] Habermas views law as playing a critical role as an intermediary among the elements of the lifeworld and the overall system. Law is the mechanism or vehicle that distributes or circulates norms among constituent elements of the social world.[83] While by no means the same as Durkheim's somewhat simplistic concept of law as the means of sustaining the conscience collective, the theoretical concepts are clearly related especially as between the maintenance of social cohesiveness and the mechanism of law as a device to communicate norms. In this respect, it is important to keep in mind that communicative activity seems to always play a key role in Habermas's analysis. To the extent that sustaining the social cohesion by memorialising norms as formal laws is conceptually congruent with law as the means of communicating norms, the Durkheim-Habermas relationship is harmonious, if not quite the same. Habermas, of course, has the distinct advantage of writing from the perspective of post–World War II Europe whereas Durkheim's first work, *The Division of Labor in Society,* was written in the nineteenth century before the social ructions of the twentieth century.

Treading a narrow course between giving too much detail and being guilty of picking and choosing so selectively as to distort essential meanings, any type of summary of Habermas's writings is a daunting task. However, because of his continuing focus on communication, concepts can be extrapolated to develop a free speech theory. In this respect, the arguments presented here are perhaps best described as abbreviated summary of extremely intricate theory.

Habermas believed that society is a medium inhabited by its residents. This reflects (1) Weber's social view that society is the aggregate of the individuals who comprise it, (2) Durkheim's belief that society is an entity unto itself consisting of its inhabitants but is a distinct organism that cannot be defined as the sum of the organisms dwelling within it and, (3)Talcott Parson's additional factor that society also includes the effect of individuals acting upon each other. Of particular interest in a freedom of expression analysis, Habermas attributes social action as being coordinated by speech or language use. In this critical respect, Habermas, far more than Durkheim, employs his theory to directly approach freedom of speech. In his magnum opus, entitled *The Theory of Communicative Action*[84] Habermas stated that the primary function of speech is the coordination of actions of the majority of individuals which allows for conflict free society:[85]

> Processes of reaching understanding aim at an agreement that meets the conditions of rationally motivated assent to the content of an utterance. A communicatively achieved agreement has a rational basis; it cannot be imposed by either party, whether instrumentally through intervention in the situation directly or strategically through influencing the decisions of opponents. Agreement can indeed be objectively obtained by force; but what comes to pass manifestly through outside influence or the use of violence cannot count subjectively as agreement. Agreement rests on common convictions. The speech act of one person succeeds only if the other accepts the offer contained in it by taking (however implicitly) a 'yes' or 'no' position on a validity claim with his utterance that is in principle criticisable.[86]

As noted in this passage, Habermas employed the term "validity claim." This concept is an essential aspect of his philosophy in the same way as organic solidarity is central to Durkheim's model. As used by Habermas, whenever human agents use language to coordinate their actions, they enter into certain commitments to justify their actions or words on the basis of good reasons. These reasons are termed "validity claims."[87]

The concept of validity claims bears comparison with Durkheim's concept of the transition from mechanical to organic solidarity. Durkheim envisaged mechanical solidarity to be the social condition where religious and traditional shared values predominated and there was little division of labour. As division of labour became the rule rather than the exception, shared values became less commonplace and criminal sanctions diminished as disputes became less a matter of generally antisocial behaviour and more a matter of private contractual controversy. Habermas believed that the communicated validity claims made by members of modern society provide for social stability without shared moral values, religious traditions, or threats of punishment.[88] In Durkheim's terms, mechanical solidarity is replaced by organic solidarity which Habermas sees as typified by society in which individual actions are coordinated by speech—speech in which validity claims are articulated. These validity claims are the fabric of social cohesion as they define the relationship between individuals:

> From the perspective of a hearer to whom an utterance is addressed, we can distinguish three levels of reaction to a (correctly perceived) speech act: The hearer understands the utterance, that is, he grasps the meaning of what is said; with his "yes" or "no" the hearer takes a position on the claim raised with the speech act, that is, he accepts the speech act offer or declines it; and in consequence of an achieved agreement, the hearer directs his action according to conventionally fixed obligations.[89]

If the validity claim is accepted by the listener, consensus is attained. However, this is frequently not the case and the speaker must defend the statements in the validity claim. Using Habermas's methodology, this moves the process towards discourse. The rules of discourse cannot exist without freedom of expression. The rules of discourse require that:

> 1. Every subject [human being] with the competence to speak and act is allowed to take part in the discourse.

2. a) Everyone is allowed to question any assertion whatsoever.

b) Everyone is allowed to introduce any assertion whatsoever into the discourse.

c) Everyone is allowed to express his attitudes, desires and needs.

3. No speaker may be prevented by internal or external coercion, from exercising his rights as laid down in (1) and (2) above.[90]

Habermas used the concepts of validity claims and discourse to establish the basis of modern social order. He postulated that modern, secular societies' social order relies on communicative action consisting of validity claims and discourse used to forge consensus that binds society together.[91] An exciting aspect of this social analysis is that validity claims and, especially discourse, absolutely and clearly require a broad grant of freedom of expression. Again, as in Durkheim's more basic model, freedom of speech is a function of modern society and does not require specific justification. It is simply required to create a functional society where not everyone shares exactly the same beliefs, ideas, perspectives and experiences.

Both Durkheim and Habermas saw freedom of expression as an essential requirement for life in modern, complex societies. Interestingly, both regarded freedom of expression operating most effectively among small groups that share certain affinity. Habermas is focused on the need for consensus and he viewed small groups as the most effective mechanism. Habermas found significance in phenomena as basic as coffee house conversations. Durkheim also envisaged small groups as the means to bringing harmony or solidarity to organic society but he focused on more formal groupings. As division of labour continues to increase, the apparent disorganisation of the economic aspects of life increase, and Durkheim believed that there was a need for some mechanism whereby similarly situated competing persons could harmonise their activities. He envisioned that a possible mechanism to provide some level of unity and ethics would be found in affinity groups such as professional societies, trade unions, or other occupational groupings.[92] These groups would provide essential unity and, most of all, moral authority for the individual and would effectively mediate the relationship between the individual and the larger society and the state.[93] This view, while somewhat idealistic, finds modern application in the concept of the political interest group whereby similarly situated individuals or businesses can be effective in society as a whole by communicating common needs and concerns. This point was also articulated by American politician and US Attorney General Elliot Richardson in his defence of political lobbying:

> If individuals didn't have professional associations, labour unions, veterans organisations, Audubon societies, taxpayer federations, the American Association of Retired Persons, and a host of other groups to champion their interests, how would they have a chance of being heard?[94]

As division of labour increases, the processes of individuation and autonomy also advance as individuals no longer see the world through the same perspective. For the gears of this differentiated society to mesh, the individuals must develop a mechanism to coordinate their activities and their relations with each other. Habermas argued that communicative action and discourse are the means to the end, which is agreement or consensus.

Habermas viewed the mechanism for reaching consensus as perhaps emanating from something more intimate than the professional association or trade union. Habermas believed that consensus was the key to the happy life and that consensus could only be reached when communication was free and open and not distorted by one speaker exerting coercive power over other speakers. By each participant having full opportunity to listen and speak, he envisaged that the best argument would prevail.[95] As will be seen in the chapter on classical speech theory, Habermas's conclusion about consensus bears close comparison to John Stuart Mill's nineteenth-century argument that truth will emerge if ideas, both valid and dubious, are permitted to collide freely in open debate. Habermas maintained that civil society requires a public sector that mediates between government and the private sector. These public spheres include everything from coffee houses to party assemblies, church congresses and even rock concerts.[96] For the public sphere to effectively operate to facilitate civil society, Habermas said that freedom of expression is essential:

> Freedom of the press, radio and television, as well as the right to engage in these areas, safeguards the media infrastructure of public communication; such liberties are thereby supposed to preserve an openness for competing opinions and a representative diversity of voices. The political system, which must remain sensitive to the influence of public opinion, is intertwined with the public sphere and civil society through the activity of political parties and general elections. This intermeshing is guaranteed by the right of parties to collaborate in the political will-formation of the people....[97]

Habermas saw civil society as the non-governmental associations and organisations that distil societal problems and transmit them to the larger public society.[98] This bears close similarity to Durkheim's affinity groups such as professional organisations or trade unions. Habermas has vastly expanded the type of mechanism from Durkheim's rather formal list to include more temporary associations. For these mechanisms to work, Habermas argued that freedom of expression must flourish.

From the sociological point of view, freedom of speech in all its forms is a function of modern society. If this is the case, the various legal and philosophical explanations are then best viewed as theory underlying, informing, and supporting sociological reality. The sociological argument accommodates all or virtually all of the philosophical theories. Even the free speech theory based on American distrust of government is anticipated by Durkheim. For Durkheim, democracy is a social mechanism by which laws can be "debated and legal-moral ideas can be communicated and developed" and "democracy is made necessary by the nature of modern morality." [99] Most importantly, the sociological approach provides sound theory for justifying regional interpretations of legal theories that on their face brook no variations. The very heart of sociological analysis is examination of local population; sociology presumes that differences exist and tries to understand those differences. In terms of free speech, it is well recognised that different societies place different values on freedom of speech because of local cultural values.[100]

How does the sociological approach fare in real-world situations? Perhaps it is helpful to consider two important and dissimilar aspects of speech—political and commercial in several different national settings. In the United States, both commercial and political speech are relatively unhindered. This is predicted if Durkheim's concept of organic solidarity is applied because in both situations, there is substantial individualisation among members of society and very little in the way of uniform thought. In the commercial context, there are typically numerous manufacturers and suppliers of similar products. At first glance, the means of distribution seem quite chaotic as there is no regulatory agency determining allocations of resources. The entire process from natural resources extraction through research and development is a seeming hodgepodge of individual action among autonomous parties. Yet, there is indeed a working system by which steel is produced in sufficient quantities to satisfy manufacturing needs and manufacturers produce sufficient goods to satisfy the retail trade and consumers. Adam Smith and his followers sometimes refer to this process as the invisible hand, but it can also be viewed as a function of freedom of commercial speech necessitated by organic solidarity and the division of labour.

In a primitive society consisting solely of hunter-gatherers, there is no commercial activity because everyone is engaged in the exact same subsistence activity. The society can function without speech. However, as the division of labour increases, each constituent element of society becomes separate and more individuated. Perhaps contrary to the so-called invisible hand approach, Durkheim would posit that there is nothing invisible or mysterious at all about how such a differentiated society functions—the individual elements coordinate their activities through communication or, in Habermas's terms, communicative action and discourse. Through communication, organic solidarity presents as smoothly running a society as the more primitive case of mechanical solidarity where everyone is engaged in the same activity.

In the context of political speech, countries such as Australia, Canada, England, and the United States allow for relatively unfettered debate concerning candidates for elective office. Using the sociological model, this can be predicted as not being simply a desirable state of affairs so much as it is an essential state of affairs and integral to the system of government itself. The right to freedom of speech flows from the government system itself—it is not an independent value. A comparison to contemporary North Korea where political debate serves absolutely no useful purpose in the context of the absolute totalitarian government makes this point clearer. To allow political debate in the context of a state where the individuals have no stake in the selection of leaders would result in a condition where the laws are not harmonious with community values. This statement is not made to validate the North Korean government but rather it is offered to point out that the relative absence of freedom of speech in North Korea is harmonious with the norms or values of the society itself. In Durkheim's terms, government in North Korea reflects mechanical solidarity—completely shared beliefs with no room for individualism. The question of the suitability of such a repressive government is a matter of human rights and politics. However, expansion of political freedom of speech rights is not conducive to the smooth running of the current North Korean political society. In fact, expanded freedom of speech could be quite disruptive to the society.

However, the absence of freedom of speech with respect to economic affairs in North Korea has resulted in catastrophic results including famine and profound misallocation of resources. In many respects, North Korea is a modern industrial state exhibiting substantial division of labour within the economic sphere. The division of labour precludes mechanical solidarity—to function, the economy requires freedom of expression. The development of a nuclear industry is dramatic proof of well-established division of labour in the economy. Yet, freedom of speech within the economy is as curtailed as it is within the political environment. This has certainly contributed to the massive failings within the North Korean economic sector. Division of labour requires freedom of speech but the legal environment is highly restrictive even within the economic sphere. The use of totally centralised controls to mediate the economy has failed in North Korea as it has failed in all industrial states where it has been attempted. This can be contrasted with China where political speech is restricted but economic speech flourishes as does the commercial economy.

In contrast, the liberal democracies present an entirely different situation. Restriction of political speech along the lines practiced in North Korea would result in an unsustainable social condition with the laws out of synch with the needs of society. In Australia, for example, the public votes for federal, state, and local leaders. Normally there are multiple individuals seeking election for each office. Individuals must make a selection and this would simply not be possible without rights of communication and free expression among the candidates, the media, and the public. Freedom of speech is a function of the democratic process itself. Just as in the commercial context, there is no invisible hand guiding elections, there is far-ranging political discourse leading to consensus.

CONCLUSION

The sociological analysis of freedom of speech fundamentally differs from explanations based on legal theory or philosophy because, viewed through the sociological lens, freedom of speech is not an option but a requirement of modern democratic society. Freedom of speech is both a cause and a consequence of social systems. It is a function of the individualisation caused by the division of labour in society. Sociology may not explain the virtues of free speech but is more conclusionary—society requires it to function. As the group becomes more of a collection of autonomous beings each fulfilling a more specific role, communication is essential or the social organism can no longer function.

ENDNOTES

1. See, for example, Jeremy Lipschultz, *Free Expression in the Age of the Internet: Social and Legal Boundaries*, 79–96, 173–197.
2. Roger Cotterrell, *Law, Culture and Society: Legal Ideas in the Mirror of Social Theory*, 1.
3. See Martin Redish, "The Value of Free Speech" (1981–1982) 130 *University of Pennsylvania Law Review* 591, 593–596.
4. J. Harris, *Legal Philosophies*, 262.
5. William Ewald, "Comparative Jurisprudence (I): What Was It Like To Try a Rat?" (1995) 143 *University of Pennsylvania Law Review* 1889, 2019–2020.
6. Vincenzo Zeno-Zencovich, *Freedom of Expression—A Critical and Comparative Analysis*, 125.
7. Jerome Skolnick, "Foreword: The Sociological Tort of Defamation" (1986) 74 *California Law Review* 677. See also, Robert Post, "The Social Foundations of Defamation Law: Reputation and the Constitution" (1986) 74 *California Law Review* 691 (discusses three aspects of community reputation or social relationships).
8. Lyrissa Lidsky, "Defamation, Reputation and the Myth of Community" (1996) 71 *Washington Law Review* 1, 14.
9. Skolnick.
10. Alan Hunt, *The Sociological Movement in Law*, 1–10.
11. Ibid., 1.
12. Ibid., 7.
13. Ibid., 136.
14. Ibid., 137. Professor Hunt provides a very clear explanation of the development of the sociological movement in law: at 134–151.
15. Roger Cotterrell, *The Sociology of Law*, 107.
16. Hunt, 139.
17. Bryan Turner, "Preface to the Second Edition" in Emile Durkheim, *Professional Ethics and Social Morals*, xiii.
18. Hunt, 147.
19. Ibid., 151. Professor Hunt maintained however that the more complex theoretical framework devised by Weber provides a more comprehensive treatment of the sociology of law: at 138.

20. Mustafa Emirbayer (ed), *Emile Durkheim: Sociologist of Modernity*, 1. A comprehensive biographical study of Durkheim's work is contained in Steven Lukes, *Emile Durkheim: His Life and Work, A Historical and Critical Study*.
21. Maria Serafimova, Stephen Hunt and Mario Marinov (eds), *Sociology and Law: The 150th Anniversary of Emile Durkheim (1858–1917)*, 1.
22. Throughout this discussion, the primary source will be the 1984 translation of *The Division of Labor in Society* (*Division of Labor*): Emile Durkheim, *The Division of Labor in Society* (W. Halls trans, New York: Free Press, 1984). However, almost all of the material cited can also be found in slightly different form in an anthology of Durkheim's works selected and translated by Anthony Giddens: Emile Durkheim, *Selected Writings* (Anthony Giddens trans, Cambridge, New York: Cambridge University Press, 1972). Where possible, citations to the Giddens selections will be provided following the citation to the Halls translation.
23. Robert Jones, *Emile Durkheim: An Introduction to Four Major Works*, 18.
24. Emile Durkheim, "The Materialist Conception of History" (1897) 44 *Revue Philosophique* 645–651, translated in Emile Durkheim, *The Rules of the Sociological Method and Selected Texts on Sociology and Its Method*, 167-174 and Giddens, 159–162 (This article was Durkheim's review of Antonio Labriola's book concerning historical materialism). See generally, Emile Durkheim, *The Elementary Forms of Religious Life*. On this point, perhaps Weber ultimately had the better argument because he maintained that it was naïve and counterproductive to try to reduce social transformations to a single cause. See Dragan Milovanovic, *An Introduction to the Sociology of Law*, 47.
25. Ken Morrison, *Marx, Durkheim, Weber–Formations of Modern Social* Thought, 313–327.
26. Durkheim, *The Rules of the Sociological Method*, 174.
27. Durkheim, *Division of Labor*, 17–23.
28. Hunt, , Ch. 4 "Emile Durkheim–Towards a Sociology of Law", 74.
29. Durkheim, *Division of Labor*, 39; Giddens, 123–124.
30. Ibid., 40; Giddens, 123–124.
31. Ibid., 44; Giddens, 124. The colonial American punishment of tongue boring would certainly satisfy this quality of repressive punishment, which is, suffering for the sake of suffering without tangible benefit to the victim of the libel.
32. Ibid., 57–58; Giddens, 127.
33. Milovanovic, *An Introduction to the Sociology of Law*, 31–32.

34. Durkheim, *Division of Labor,* 68; Giddens, 135.
35. Ibid., 71; Giddens, 137.
36. Ibid., 71; Giddens, 136.
37. Jones, 19.
38. Ibid., 25. See Milovanovic, 29–30. Durkheim acknowledged that law only furnishes an incomplete picture of social facts and is sometimes not current with the social condition.
39. Roger Cotterrell, *Emile Durkheim: Law in a Moral Domain*, 12–17.
40. Serafimova, Hunt & Marinov.
41. See Emile Durkheim, *Contributions to L'Annee Sociologique.*
42. John Hughes, Wes Sharrock & Peter Martin, *Understanding Classical Sociology: Marx, Weber, Durkheim*, 215–216. See Emile Durkheim, *On Suicide.*
43. See Hughes, Sharrock & Martin, vii. See also, Craig Calhoun et al (eds), *Contemporary Sociological Theory*, 1.
44. There exists a significant literature that continues to evaluate Durkheim's contributions to modern sociology. See, for example, William Pickering, *Durkheim Today* and Ivan Strenski, *The New Durkheim*. There is also the British Centre for Durkheimian Studies based at Oxford University and a journal, *Durkheimian Studies*. However, there seems to be little current attention focused on legal aspects of Durkheim's theories. In a more light-hearted vein, a "new" Sherlock Holmes novel introduces readers to classical sociology theory with particular deference to Durkheim and Weber as the central characters in the story. See Arthur Berger, *Durkheim is Dead! Sherlock Holmes Is Introduced to Social Theory*, 38–43.
45. For example, Durkheim and Weber receive more attention and discussion than other sociologists in two recent texts concerning law and sociology. See A. Javier Trevino, *The Sociology of Law* (Durkheim and Weber occupy 36% of this 440-page work) and Mathieu Deflem, *Sociology of Law.*
46. Steven Lukes and Andrew Scull, *Durkheim and the Law,* 1. This book is a significant undertaking because it reflects the efforts of two recognised Durkheim scholars to compile all of Durkheim's own discussions of the law from his books and articles to form a coherent single text which amounts to a unitary work dealing with law.
47. Ibid.
48. Ronald Dworkin, "Lord Devlin and the Enforcement of Morals" *Yale Law Journal* 75 (1965–1966): 986, 987. While Devlin's arguments are

contained in a number of works, Professor Dworkin provides a comprehensive summary in this article.

49. H.L.A. Hart, "Social Solidarity and the Enforcement of Morality" *University of Chicago Law Review* 35 (1967–1968): 1.
50. Ibid., 2. See Dworkin, 986. The debate between proponents of positivism and natural law has a number of variants and tries to resolve the relationship of law to morality. See Matthew Bunker, *Critiquing Free Speech: First Amendment Theory and the Challenge of Interdisciplinarity*, 159.
51. H.L.A Hart, "Immorality and Treason" in Ronald Dworkin (ed), *The Philosophy of Law*, 83, 85.
52. Hart, 'Social Solidarity', 13.
53. Ibid., 1.
54. Ibid., 5.
55. Ibid., 8.
56. Cotterrell, *Emile Durkheim: Law in a Moral Domain,* ix.
57. Hart, "Immorality and Treason", 87–88.
58. See Alexander Hamilton, James Madison, and John Jay, *The Federalist Papers*.
59. Hart, "Social Solidarity", 6.
60. Cotterrell, [*Emile Durkheim: Law in a Moral* Domain]33–34.
61. Hunt, *The Sociological Movement in Law*, 69.
62. Durkheim, *Division of Labor,* above n 22, 108–109.
63. It should also be noted that empirical support for what Hart termed the disintegration thesis perhaps exists in the history of Puritans in colonial America. See W. John Thomas, "Social Solidarity and the Enforcement of Morality Revisited: Some Thoughts on H.L.A. Hart's Critique of Durkheim" (1994–1995) 32 *American Criminal Law Review* 49, 58–64.
64. Trevino, *The Sociology of Law*, 238.
65. Michael Clarke, "Durkheim's Sociology of Law" (1976) 3 *British Journal of Law & Society* 246, 250–254.
66. See Jones, 58.
67. Lukes, 168–169; Trevino, 238.
68. Durkheim, *Division of Labor*, 205 (italics in original).
69. For a detailed discussion of historical studies in which Durkheim's theoretical arguments find support and the limitations of that evidence, see Trevino, 241–271.
70. See Thomas, 58–60.
71. Durkheim, *Professional Ethics and Civic Morals*, 56.
72. Ibid., 90. Lukes, 272–273.

73. Lukes & Scull, 102–104.
74. Durkheim, *Professional Ethics and Civic Morals*, 91.
75. James Gordon Finlayson, *Habermas—A Very Short Introduction.*
76. Gerd Nollman, "Habermas, Jurgen" in George Ritzer (ed), *Encyclopedia of Social Theory*, vol. 1, 351–352.
77. Finlayson, 51–52.
78. Ibid. 53–54.
79. Ibid. 56.
80. Nollman, 351.
81. Ibid.
82. Lukes and Scull, 1.
83. Nollman, 352.
84. Jurgen Habermas, volumes 1 and 2, *The Theory of Communicative Action,* Thomas McCarthy trans. (*"TCA").*
85. Finlayson, 34.
86. Habermas, *TCA* vol. 1, 287
87. Finlayson, 26.
88. Ibid., 27.
89. Habermas, *TCA* vol. 1, 297.
90. Finlayson, 43. Jurgen Habermas, *Moral Consciousness and Communicative Action,* 89.
91. Finlayson, 47.
92. Hughes, Sharrock, and Martin, 193–194.
93. Ibid.
94. Elliot Richardson, *Reflections of a Radical Moderate*, 22.
95. See George Ritzer, *Contemporary Social Theory & Its Classical* Roots, 129-130.
96. Jurgen Habermas, "Civil Society and the Public Political Sphere' [1966], in Craig Calhoun et al (eds), *Contemporary Social Theory*, 398.
97. Ibid., 394.
98. Ibid., 393.
99. Cotterrell, *Emile Durkheim: Law in a Moral Domain*, 160.
100. Ian Cram, *Contested Words: Legal Restrictions on Freedom of Speech in Liberal Democracies*, 12–13, 31–32.

Chapter 3

The Continuing Relevance of Durkheim

The Demise of Criminal Defamation

Unlike philosophy, which, by its nature, may not be easily susceptible to empirical testing, sociological theory should be capable of validation or rejection through empirical testing because sociology as a discipline is frequently reliant on empirical evidence. Nevertheless, it is difficult to measure human behaviour reliably outside of carefully controlled laboratory conditions. Since one of the subjects of this book is free speech based on century-old social theory, it is probative to show that Durkheim's concept of organic solidarity and its consequences can find validation in the actual evolution of laws relating to freedom of speech. The evolution of criminal libel in the United States and England from a Durkheimian perspective will be examined as a case in point. This relates to Durkheim's second legal hypothesis that as society moves from mechanical towards organic solidarity, the tendency of the law will be to move from penal sanctions representing a breach of commonly held values and toward restitutive sanctions representing a breach of individual interests. This hypothesis is an essential aspect of organic solidarity where individual autonomy supplants universally held beliefs.

Defamation is generally described as written or oral statements made about someone that tend to diminish the reputation of that person in the estimation of right-thinking or ordinary decent members of society.[1] Traditionally, the law of defamation included both criminal and civil remedies. However, recent legislation abolished criminal defamation in England altogether.[2] Within the United States, First Amendment concerns make the continued viability of criminal defamation a dubious proposition. In addition to legislation and constitutional issues, empirical evidence demonstrates that even with the enormous increase in populations over the past three hundred years, criminal libel virtually disappeared in both the United States and England. Although recently developed empirical evidence from one American state (Wisconsin) may indicate an upswing in criminal libel prosecutions, this is likely only a localised and temporary aberration and does not reflect any ill-advised trend in the US to resurrect this archaic doctrine.

While criminal defamation historically had any number of local idiosyncrasies that varied among jurisdictions—and although there are differences between the tort and crime of defamation—the general principles are reasonably similar.[3] While some of the historical reasons may have differed, criminal libel has evolved so that its underlying rationale is difficult to distinguish from tortious libel.[4] Consequently, the abolition of criminal defamation is not so much a change in substantive law as it is a change, albeit a radical one, in the availability of remedies. The abolition or slow extinction of criminal libel is difficult to explain through traditional free speech theory because the demise of criminal libel does not expand or detract from permissible speech; it only affects whether the remedy for impermissible speech is public (criminal) or private (civil damages) law. The sociological approach, however, offers a clear analytical explanation for the demise of criminal defamation in the context of social forces.

Application of Traditional Free Speech Theory

An alteration in the available remedies for defamation, unlike a change in the subject matter or type of speech constituting actionable defamation, is challenging to accommodate within the free speech theoretical landscape. By merely eliminating criminal penalties, free speech is not necessarily promoted unless there is a simultaneous elimination of restitutionary remedies. The consequence is that the logic for abolishing criminal defamation based solely on elimination of criminal penalties is difficult to support through free speech theory alone. However, to the extent that there are substantive types of speech prohibited by criminal libel laws that do not attract civil libel liability, then free speech theory may also provide a rationale for the elimination of criminal libel. In other words, abolition of criminal libel does not promote free speech unless it liberates types of speech that are not also barred by the tort. But, as will be shown, a change in remedy can be supported sociologically.

Historically, criminal libel existed to keep the peace, maintain the existing hierarchy, and promote harmony in society. Keeping the peace and promoting harmony was really a euphemism for the deterrence of duelling, and maintaining the existing hierarchy meant deterring criticism of powerful people in leadership positions, usually the aristocracy or the Crown. Publication to third parties was irrelevant to preventing duelling and therefore criminal libel did not require publication to a third party. Contrary to the law of civil defamation, defaming the dead was actionable because the offence was not to the reputation of the individual but to the ruling order and to defame someone's ancestors might constitute a challenge to the existing social hierarchy. However, the primary distinction with civil libel was that truth was not a defence to criminal libel. Historically, the major factors present in common law criminal libel that distinguished it from civil defamation were:

An action could be maintained for defaming the deceased.[5]

Publication to third parties was not required.

Truth was not a defence.[6]

Had these aspects of criminal libel survived to the present day, it is reasonably clear that abolition of the crime would in fact facilitate free speech that is not otherwise prohibited by civil tort law.

However, with the passage of time, the legal aspects of criminal libel evolved to the point of substantially overlapping with the civil tort. For example, the criminal offence of defaming the dead appears to prohibit defamatory speech concerning an enormous range of subjects—namely, everyone who is deceased. But, actions for defaming the dead were relegated to the legal curiosity bin long ago. Evidence suggests there were no such prosecutions in the US subsequent to World War I and even before that, there were only a handful, including one in 1916 where an individual published some unkind words about George Washington in a local newspaper.[7] The malicious words about the father of his country were published only four days before the Washington Birthday holiday. The accused argued that since no member of Washington's immediate family could possibly be alive in 1916 that there was not any risk of public disturbance and that there had to be some limitation of time after which the dead would be fair game. The Supreme Court of Washington affirmed the conviction and noted that at common law there was likely some limitation after which the rights of the dead could not form the basis of prosecution but the law of the State of Washington recognised no such limitation.[8] It would seem that under Washington law, impugning the virtue of Cleopatra might have also landed the offender in prison.

The absence of requiring publication to a third party in criminal libel also appears to be a distinction without a difference. In every reported American case after 1920, there was not an instance in which the issue of publication would have made a difference because in all but two cases there had been publication to third parties, and in those two cases in which publication was absent, the charges were dismissed because there had not been adequate publication.[9]

While the first two of the differentiating factors may be of historical interest only, the issue of truth as a defence is extremely important. In civil defamation cases, truth has long been recognised as an absolute defence at common law.[10] However, because individual reputation in the community was not the key issue in criminal libel, truth was not a defence. Criminal libel was concerned with maintaining public order, and a true statement could indeed do more to disturb the peace than a falsehood—the greater the truth, the greater the libel:[11] "truth was irrelevant; in fact the true insult was considered more likely to give offense for, as the woman said, she would never grieve to be told of her red nose if she had not one indeed."[12] The absence of truth as a defence appears to constitute a significant curtailment of freedom of speech. In traditional free speech theory terminology, if speaking the truth can amount to a punishable crime, both the marketplace of ideas and the discovery of truth are likely to be impaired rather dramatically. After all, how can there be speech with the goal of discovering the truth if speaking the truth may result in criminal conviction? Similarly, such a restriction would even taint the constitutive justification for freedom of speech—how can self-fulfilment or autonomy be achieved if speaking the truth may land the speaker in trouble with the law? Again, twenty-first century reality differs from the traditional rule.

In 1964, the US Supreme Court made landmark rulings in both civil and criminal defamation cases. In *New York Times v. Sullivan*,[13] First Amendment considerations were imposed on civil defamation actions involving public official complainants (later expanded to include all public figures). The Court held that the First Amendment required, among other things, that in cases involving public officials, complainants prove by clear and convincing evidence that the defendant either had actual knowledge of falsity or acted in reckless disregard of the truth when publishing the defamatory statement. Seven months thereafter, in a less well-known decision, the Supreme Court was called upon to scrutinise the validity of

Louisiana's criminal libel laws in *Garrison v. Louisiana.*[14] In *Garrison,* the local District Attorney, who achieved dubious fame or notoriety for conducting the only criminal prosecution in connection with the assassination of President John Kennedy, had accused eight New Orleans judges of being lazy, taking excessive vacations, and being sympathetic to purveyors of vice. Truth was not a defence under Louisiana law. In response to the District Attorney's statements, the judges charged him with criminal libel. He was convicted by the local court and the conviction was affirmed by the Supreme Court of Louisiana.

In striking down the Louisiana law as being constitutionally inconsistent with *New York Times,* the US Supreme Court employed language that reads as if Durkheim was offering his sociological explanation for the transition from criminal to civil law. The Court said:

> Changing mores and the virtual disappearance of criminal libel prosecutions lend support to the observation that…under modern conditions, when the rule of law is generally accepted as a substitute for private physical measures, it can hardly be urged that the maintenance of peace requires a criminal prosecution for private defamation.[15]

After making this observation, the Supreme Court proceeded to find the Louisiana law constitutionally infirm because it did not allow truth as an absolute defence and did not meet the minimal standards for a civil defamation case concerning public officials as established in *New York Times.*[16]

More recently, in 2008, the Washington Court of Appeals struck down that State's criminal libel law as being unconstitutional.[17] Allan Parmelee was an inmate in a Washington State prison who wrote a letter in which he referred to the prison superintendent as a "man-hater lesbian." He was charged with a misdemeanour under a criminal libel law that had been hibernating since 1925, which made it a crime punishable by fine and imprisonment to publish words that "expose any living person to hatred, contempt, ridicule…." The only permissible defence was that the statement was true and published "with good motives and for justifiable ends."[18] The Washington Court held that the statute was unconstitutional because it neither required actual malice (knowledge of falsity) nor was truth alone an absolute defence.[19] The Washington Court might have salvaged the statute by reading into the statute the constitutional requirements established in *Garrison;* most specifically that truth is an absolute defence.[20] However, since the *Garrison* Court in 1964 had made specific mention of the Washington statute as being constitutionally infirm, as one of twenty five states impermissibly permitting common law malice (ill-will or spite) to vitiate the availability of truth as a defence,[21] and the state of Washington chose not to revise the statute; there would not seem to have been any reason for the Washington Court to make a special effort to salvage a law that was known to be partially invalid for over forty years. In addition, at least one state court has held that introducing substantive law changes, such as requiring actual malice in lieu of common law malice, into a statute is beyond the proper role of the courts and belongs exclusively with the legislature.[22]

Although in 2012, there are still states that have statutes that do not even conform to *Garrison's* minimal requirements, it can be assumed that those laws, if tested, would meet the same fate as the Washington law. For example, under the Oklahoma statute, truth is not a defence to criminal libel unless the publication was made with "good motives and justifiable ends." At the very least, this section of the Oklahoma criminal libel laws is clearly and unambiguously deficient under *Garrison.*[23]

For forty-five years, as a result of *Garrison*, proof of actual malice and truth as an absolute defence have been constitutionally required to sustain criminal libel charges in the United States in cases involving public officials and public figures. However, this does not resolve the issue regarding the availability of truth as an absolute defence because *Garrison* did not deal with purely private disputes not involving public people, and the application of *Garrison's* holding to purely private disputes has never reached the Supreme Court. While there exists very limited empirical evidence quantifying the number or percentage of criminal defamation proceedings that do not involve public figure situations, a recent study of criminal libel prosecutions in Wisconsin over a sixteen-year period indicates that up to79% of the disputes fell outside the reach of *Garrison*.[24] At first glance, the Wisconsin data appears to offer some support to the argument that abolition of criminal libel would substantively increase avenues of free speech because truth was not a defence to the crime. However, such a conclusion is probably misplaced because truth may be a defence to criminal defamation in Wisconsin despite the plain language of the statute.

On its face, under Wisconsin criminal defamation law, truth is not an absolute defence. Truth is only a qualified privilege that can be defeated by common law malice (spite or ill will).[25] However, the Supreme Court of Wisconsin in 2009, in an identity fraud case, noted that in a prosecution for criminal libel, the State "must show that the statement was false if a private citizen is being defamed."[26] While only *dicta* and not an essential part of the decision, this statement by the Supreme Court of Wisconsin is sufficiently clear and unambiguous to be entitled to substantial deference by that State's lower courts and likely reflects the true state of Wisconsin law. Of course, if the prosecution must prove falsity of the statement, truth need not be a separate defence. By analogy to another Wisconsin statute, proof of falsity may be an essential element. A criminal statute directed against persons giving false information to a publisher with the intent of injuring "any" person, specifically requires that the person providing the information must act "with knowledge that it [the information] is false."[27] Although not entirely clear, the situation in Wisconsin appears to substitute an affirmative prosecutorial duty to prove falsity in place of the truth defence with the result being about the same as the legal standards in American civil defamation proceedings.

Based on the state of American law, abolition of criminal libel might not meaningfully advance free speech because the quirky features unique to criminal libel have already disappeared or have been greatly ameliorated in practice. Without belabouring the point, it is helpful to look at the situation in England at least with respect to truth as an absolute defence because the situation is slightly clearer. Truth was not an absolute defence to criminal libel, but it was a partial defence under limited circumstances. Under English law, truth was a complete defence to a charge of criminal libel "if the defendant can prove that it was for the public benefit that the matters charged should be published."[28] Unfortunately, there are no authorities defining the term "public benefit."[29] Consequently, while truth is not an absolute defence in all situations, it might be a defence in situations roughly similar to the scope of *Garrison's* holding that truth is an absolute defence in cases concerning a public person. While it is tempting to conclude that abolition of criminal libel would expand free speech in England to the extent that the defence of truth was not previously available, such a conclusion is possibly unwarranted. Under the emerging tort of invasion of privacy, publication of private information can be tortious whether true or not.[30] Consequently, under English law, if the defamatory publication were for the benefit of the public, criminal defamation permitted the defence of truth. If the matter published is inherently private, criminal defamation did not permit a truth defence. The abolition of criminal libel may not change the legal landscape because the truthful publication could very well be tortious under the emerging law of invasion of privacy. Under this analysis, repeal of criminal defamation might not have any measurable impact on free speech because tort law based on privacy rights may proscribe the same conduct. If the statement were true and not of public benefit, criminal libel would have been available as a remedy under the old law; while today, invasion of privacy may be a legal remedy where there is not a substantial public interest in the otherwise truthful publication.

A SOCIOLOGICAL EXAMINATION INTO THE DEMISE OF CRIMINAL LIBEL

The Empirical Evidence

As discussed in chapter 2, Durkheim posited that the transition from criminal punishment to civil redress for similar antisocial behaviour is both inevitable and inherent in the evolution of organic solidarity found in modern complex societies as opposed to the mechanical solidarity found in less complex societies. Organic solidarity should be distinguished by a diminution in criminal or repressive sanctions and a corresponding rise in civil or restitutive remedies with respect to the same transgressions. The history of criminal defamation conforms to the sociological prediction. A modern study by Larry Eldridge of how seditious or blasphemous speech was punished in seventeenth-century colonial America, conducted to show the origins of free speech in America,[31] also demonstrates the changes over time in how colonial society punished libellous conduct.

The settlement of the American colonies began in the early seventeenth century with only a handful of settlers, but by the end of the century the colonies were substantially larger, and cities such as Boston, New York, Philadelphia, and Hartford were relatively well established. Initially, of course, the settlers were engaged in subsistence farming, but as their numbers increased and urbanisation began, there was the opportunity for greater division of labour within the population. The growth in the settlements even allowed the colonists to establish formal institutions of learning such as Harvard (1636) and Yale (1701). Contemporaneous with the growth and development of colonial society, there were also changes in the punishments handed out to those who engaged in criminal libel. Furthermore, criminal libel was not the only criminal remedy for unwarranted speech. Laws existed that provided for the public gagging of persons who engaged in excessive scolding (harsh chiding) or railing (reviling with insolent or vituperative language).[32]

In the 1620s, bodily correction, including branding, whipping, cutting of ears, tongue boring, and limb breaking, was meted out in slightly over fifty percent of libel cases.[33] Yet, by the end of the seventeenth century, these rather grotesque punishments, except for occasional lashings, had disappeared even though the population had increased dramatically and the number of libels would have also been expected to increase.[34] Even the far milder penalty of court-imposed fines showed dramatic reduction over this same period. In the 1620s in the United States, fines in excess of GBP 5 were imposed in about seventy-five percent of cases but by the 1690s, fines exceeding GBP 5 were only applied to only twenty-five percent of cases.[35]

Just as the type of punishments for criminal libel transitioned from severe imposition of physical pain to modest monetary sanctions, there was also an actual decrease in the number of criminal proceedings. Jumping to the twentieth century, based on the number of reported decisions, there has been a marked decrease in criminal defamation prosecutions in the United States. The approximate number of criminal defamation appellate decisions for each group of years is as follows:

Table 1. Approximate number of criminal defamation appellate decisions in the United States.

Years	Cases Reported
1897–1906	98
1907–1916	93
1920–1929	58
1930–1941	34
1942–1955	18

Source. Robert Leflar, "The Social Utility of the Criminal Law of Defamation", *Texas Law Review* 34 (1955–1956): 984, 985.

Of the 110 cases decided between 1920 and 1955 in which there were convictions (about 50%), the punishments were not particularly severe.

Most involved only monetary fines and, of these, only one fine exceeded $750. Only a handful involved imprisonment, and merely two called for incarceration of six months or longer.[36] More recent results show a continued decline:

Table 2. Continued decline of cases reported.

Years	Cases Reported
1957–1966	19
1967–1976	19
1977–1986	10
1987–1996	5

Source. Gregory Lisby, "No Place in the Law: The Ignominy of Criminal Libel in American Jurisprudence", *Communication Law & Policy* 9 (2004): 433, 467.

These totals do not equal the precise numbers of actual prosecutions because only appellate decisions are typically reported. However, since there is not any obvious reason for the proportion of reported appeals to trials to change radically within these time periods, the numbers clearly reflect a downward trend in actual cases.

In terms of actual cases filed, as opposed to appellate decisions reported, numbers for recent years also appear to be quite small. A study found that there were sixty-one criminal libel prosecutions in Wisconsin from 1991 through 2007 and of these, only five (eight percent) reached the appellate courts and would be likely discovered as reported cases.[37] Even if the eight percent were applied to the national total of appellate decisions, this would indicate that the five reported cases between 1987 and 1996 would translate into the grand total of 63 cases over the decade. Furthermore, only fourteen states even have criminal libel laws as of 2012. There were approximately 21.5 million criminal cases filed in state courts in 2006 alone and, between 2008 and 2009, the Media Law Resource Center found only nineteen criminal defamation prosecutions, which amounts to a microscopic percentage of all criminal cases.[38] The relative number of criminal defamation cases is even more minuscule in light of the rapidly expanding population of the United States. At the beginning of the twentieth century, the US population was only 76 million and at the beginning of the twenty-first century it exceeds 300 million.

Subsequent to the *Garrison* decision in 1964, constitutional issues likely deterred some criminal prosecutions. However, *Garrison* did not outlaw criminal defamation, and it can certainly be argued that *Garrison* simply did not go far enough and failed to examine critically the basic legitimacy of criminal libel in contemporary society. It has been suggested that *Garrison* was decided on basis that was far too restricted and that the Court should have used the opportunity to abolish criminal libel on the ground that defamation is not a public wrong but is exclusively a private tort.[39] Two years after *Garrison*, in setting aside a conviction under the Kentucky criminal libel law, the Supreme Court held that the common law crime of criminal libel was invalid as being uncertain and that, at the very least, a statutory enactment was required.[40] The US Supreme Court has not taken up criminal libel since 1966, but the paucity of recent cases at all judicial levels indicates that criminal defamation may simply atrophy in the United States through prolonged lack of use or sporadic local findings of unconstitutionality.

Despite the general trend for the decline of criminal libel, there is some anecdotal evidence that indicates a potential growth area for this otherwise moribund offence. In a study of Wisconsin criminal libel prosecutions, it was determined that internet-based defamation was a major factor in criminal libel prosecutions.[41] While none of the pre-1999 cases involved the internet, almost half (45%) of the forty cases filed from 1999 through 2007 were internet related.[42] In terms of annual prosecutions, the average number of criminal libel cases in Wisconsin from 1991 to 2007 was 2.5 cases per year, not including the internet-related cases. However, when the internet-related cases are added to the post-1998 prosecutions, the average number of prosecutions jumps to 4.44 cases per year.[43] While these numbers are very small, they do indicate that internet-related cases are not replacing traditional media cases but rather supplementing the existing volume of cases.

With respect to the internet, it is important to recognise that arguments have been raised that criminal libel is a potentially useful mechanism to control internet defamation in the United States. Under Section 230(c) of the *Communications Decency Act of 1996,*[44] internet service providers (ISP) are not considered to be publishers of third-party content.[45] With the potential ISP defendant statutorily immunised, claimants are often left with the none-too-attractive option of pursuing blogger defendants who are frequently without means to respond in damages to civil lawsuits. It has been suggested that criminal libel may present an effective means of deterring and punishing impecunious defendants[46] and, for this reason, the criminal option might constitute a means of controlling defamation on the internet.[47] However, it is difficult to imagine that busy prosecutors will have the time to engage in many criminal libel prosecutions. It should also be noted that some of the internet-based prosecutions also include charges of stalking and harassment that fall within other criminal laws and which are ultimately more appropriate.[48] Furthermore, as seen in the case discussed next, a prosecutor undoubtedly wishes that she had been too busy to get involved in a criminal libel case.

Although decided as a matter of Fourth Amendment rights to be free from unreasonable searches and seizures, judicial ambivalence or even disapproval toward criminal libel prosecutions was made quite clear in a case filed by Thomas Mink against Deputy District Attorney Susan Knox in the State of Colorado.[49] Mink was a college student who created a fictional character "Junius Puke" on his internet-based journal. A professor at the school Mink attended, Junius Peake, contacted the local police who began a criminal libel investigation. The police applied for a search warrant, which was reviewed and approved by Knox. The police carried out a search and seizure pursuant to the warrant and confiscated the computer. Mink sued in federal court for the return of his computer and was successful. Subsequently, the district attorney elected not to prosecute

Mink for criminal libel. What came next was Mink's federal claim against the deputy district attorney on the grounds that she was not protected by immunity as her approval of the search warrant was clearly unlawful under the First Amendment. The district court held that Ms Knox was protected by immunity; but on appeal, the US Court of Appeals reversed and stated unambiguously that under clear law, parody or satire could not be the basis of a defamation claim and remanded the case to the district court. On remand, the US District Court found as a matter of law that Ms Knox "violated Mr Mink's right to be free from unreasonable searches and seizures" and that he was entitled to damages.[50] In December 2011, Mr Mink reportedly accepted $425,000 to settle his claim.[51] Subsequently, legislation was passed in the Colorado legislature to repeal the criminal defamation law and on April 13, 2012, the governor signed the repeal legislation.

With *Mink v. Knox* establishing that prosecutors may become personally liable for First Amendment violations, and recognising that criminal prosecutors have their expertise outside of defamation law, it is unlikely that many prosecutors will want to follow in the footsteps of district attorney Knox and, therefore, regardless of theoretical possibilities, it is most unlikely that criminal libel will find new life because of the internet. As the Supreme Court noted in *Garrison,* defamation today is an essentially private dispute[52] and, as sociological theory suggests, in modern complex societies, restitutionary remedies are more appropriate than criminal sanctions to resolve essentially private disputes. It should also be noted that tort remedies are not limited to damages and that injunctions, although disfavoured in defamation cases, may be available to deter persistent unlawful conduct.

Although not subject to First Amendment constraints, criminal libel in England, having enjoyed a long history, has also been on the decline. Prior to its recent abolition, there were only four prosecutions between 1948 and 1975; between 1970 and 1983, there were five committals for trial; from 1984 through 1995, thirteen persons were found guilty or were cautioned, and from 1996 through 2001, only five persons were convicted or cautioned. [53] And even more recently, between 2002 and the end of 2006, only two persons were found guilty of criminal libel.[54] Part of the reason for the decline is that permission from the court must be obtained before a claim for criminal libel is pursued against a newspaper.[55] The decline became terminal when Royal Assent was given to the abolition of the crime of defamatory libel on 12 November 2009.[56]

Looking beyond England to the European Union, the legal situation is not all that different except that under European Union law, there is not an outright prohibition of prosecuting defamation as criminal activity. However, in interpreting Article 10 (freedom of expression) of the European Convention, the European Court of Human Rights in Strasbourg ("European Court") has severely limited the range of available penalties and the Court scrutinises sanctions to determine if they are justified by the offence.[57] For example, in the review of a case decided under Romanian law, the European Court held that imprisonment of journalists for reporting on matters of public interest could not be justified.[58] In *Cumpana v. Romania*, the journalists had been found to have defamed a judge by depicting her in a cartoon wearing a miniskirt revealing parts of her anatomy while walking arm-in-arm with a man holding bags of money. Neither the reporters nor their counsel appeared at the trial and the Romanian trial court sentenced the reporters to seven months of imprisonment plus a year-long disqualification as journalists and imposed a monetary fine. While the actual prison sentences were commuted by presidential pardon, the European Court still found that the nonmonetary sanctions violated Article 10 of the European Convention:

> The circumstances of the instant case, a classic case of defamation of an individual in the context of a debate on a matter of legitimate public interest, present no justification whatsoever for the imposition of a prison sentence. Such a sanction, by its very nature, will inevitably have a chilling effect, and the fact that the applicants did not serve their prison sentence does not alter that conclusion.[59]

The Court also set aside the occupational disqualification on the grounds that such a punishment "contravened the principle that the press must be able to perform the role of a public watchdog in a democratic society."[60] It also appears that some of the EU member nations are like some US states and permit criminal libel laws to remain in the statutes but keep these laws in deep freeze. For example, while criminal defamation laws continue to exist in Denmark, France, Germany, the Netherlands, Norway, and Sweden, the laws are rarely invoked against the media.[61]

Turning from Europe to the Americas, freedom of expression and respect for reputation are guaranteed by Article 13 of the *American Convention on Human Rights* ("American Convention").[62] The Inter-American Court of Human Rights ("Inter-American Court") has jurisdiction to hear disputes between individuals and signatory states under certain conditions.[63] In the course of examining national criminal libel laws in light of Article 13 of the American Convention, the Inter-American Court has reached conclusions similar to those of the European Court. While not disallowing criminal libel laws among the member states, the Inter-American Court has taken the position that criminal libel must not be applied where the publication concerns individuals involved in matters of public concern.[64] Finally, while criminal libel survives in Australia and Canada,[65] it was abolished in New Zealand.[66] In summary, while criminal libel continues to exist in many jurisdictions, the clear trend reflects its loss of favour.

Application of Sociological Theory

The historical record has demonstrated at least four changes regarding criminal libel in the United States and England. First, sanctions for criminal libel transitioned from brutal physical punishment to monetary fines which are perhaps more in the nature of civil damages except that the payment of fines is payable to the state and civil damages are paid to the injured party. Second, even as sanctions moderated, the number of prosecutions also diminished radically despite population increases. Third, criminal defamation has been abolished in England and is of questionable constitutionality in the United States. Fourth, defamation claims today are invariably resolved through civil litigation brought by private litigants and, at least in England, civil defamation is still a growth industry. Data compiled by *Media Lawyer* and *The Guardian* shows that civil defamation lawsuits filed in the Royal Courts of Justice evidence a growth trend that until very recently would be envied in most quarters of British industry:

Table 3. Civil defamation lawsuits filed in the Royal Courts of Justice.

Year	Claims Commenced	% of Claims Alleging over GBP 50,000
2011	165	36.9
2010	158	N.A.
2009	298	N.A.
2008	259	29.7
2007	233	19.3
2006	213	18.3
2005	252	27.8
2004	267	11.6
2003	190	7.9
2002	128	0.8

Source. Retrieved from http://medialawyer.press.net/article.jsp?id=8483822 and www.guardian.co.uk/news/datablog/2010/apr/15/libel-cases-general-election/print.
Note. Data for 2009 and 2010 were not available.

In the context of criminal libel, the arguments that justified the criminal treatment of defamation are very similar to Durkheim's arguments concerning the need for repressive sanctions in cultures where mechanical solidarity prevails. The primary function of criminal libel was social order and control.[67] The criminal penalty affirms the values of the conscience collective. Conversely, the purpose of civil libel is the restoration of individual reputation through the payment of damages.[68] So, there is typically the same wrongful conduct but the criminal and civil remedies are designed for different purposes. The civil tort is intended to restore parties to their prior position—it is a clear case of a restitutive remedy that Durkheim would expect to find in complex societies in which there is a substantial division of labour and a diminished collective conscience.

The empirical data concerning criminal defamation prosecutions and punishments in the United States from the earliest colonial settlements to contemporary industrial or postindustrial society clearly is in harmony with Durkheim's predicted sociological progression of law. In colonial America where there was little social division of labour and the primary occupation was subsistence farming, defamation was treated as a serious breach of community values and was punished accordingly. Mechanical solidarity was especially pronounced in the early New England colonies because of the strong religious conformity among the residents. An essential aspect of the progression from mechanical to organic solidarity is the decline in commonly held religious values and the ascendancy of secular and contractual relations. The rather brutal physical punishments of the seventeenth century reflect Durkheim's concept of mechanical solidarity to be found in less complex societies because the guilty party was made to "suffer solely for the sake of suffering and without seeking any advantage for themselves [the members of society] from the suffering" they inflicted.[69] However, as the community enlarged and engaged in a greater division of labour, the shared values diminished and treatment of libellous speech became less of a concern to the community as a whole, and criminal punishment became less severe and more infrequent.

Accepting that modern American and English society reflect a substantial social division of labour, it is not at all surprising that criminal defamation has declined. Furthermore, any attempt to resurrect criminal libel, because of the perceived inadequacy of tort law, to control internet bloggers is clearly contrary to Durkheim's theoretical paradigm. While application of criminal libel to the impecunious criminal blogger might have some superficial appeal, the temptation should be avoided because from a sociological perspective, criminal law must reflect the collective conscience of society and is not an appropriate remedy for what is still an essentially private dispute. Because of the expanded division of labour, defamatory words do not offend the collective conscience and are exclusively a private matter. To make a private matter subject to criminal law is contrary to Durkheim's concept of social cohesion and, under his paradigm; such activity undermines the legitimacy of the law itself.

As Durkheim would have predicted, criminal defamation has diminished or even disappeared as American and English societies have increasingly grown more complex. While Durkheim's theory explains the transition from criminal libel to civil defamation, this one phenomenon does not constitute a comprehensive validation of Durkheim's theoretical framework. Nevertheless, the fact that this sociological theory finds such strong application to an aspect of freedom of expression cannot be understated as support for the validity of the theory. To buttress the validity of using Durkheim as a theorist who can inform freedom of speech, it is useful to examine a more fundamental theoretical confrontation between Marx and Durkheim where, until very recently, conventional thinking did not support Durkheim. Today, however, emerging archaeological discoveries are forcing a rethinking of basic social theory concerning the rise of civilisations.

Endnotes

1. Lawrence McNamara, *Reputation and Defamation*, 31.
2. *Coroners and Justice Act (2009)* (UK) 73 (b). See also "Criminal Libel Set for Abolition", *Media Lawyer* 84 (2009): 18.
3. See Robert Leflar, "The Social Utility of the Criminal Law of Defamation", *Texas Law Review* 34 (1955 1956): 984. The Leflar article contains a comprehensive analysis of criminal libel rationales as well as a review of judicial decisions in the US up to the date of publication.
4. See Clive Walker, "Reforming the Crime of Libel" *New York Law School Law Review* 50 (2005–2006): 169, 201.
5. Verbal abuse of the dead was punishable as a crime as far back as ancient Greece. While ancient Athens recognised a right of freedom of speech, severe sanctions such as ostracism or banishment for ten years could be inflicted or threatened for socially disturbing speech. Douglas Fraleigh & Joseph Tuman, *Freedom of Speech in the Marketplace of* Ideas, 37–38.
6. Leflar, 1011–1023.
7. Ibid., 1014.
8. *State v. Hafer,* 94 Wash 136, 138–143, 162 Pac 45, 46–47 (1916).
9. Leflar, 1011.
10. Robert Sack, *Sack on Defamation: Libel Slander and Related Problems*, 3-2.
11. Ibid., citing *Tollett v. United States,* 485 F.2d 1087, 1098 fn 27 (8th Cir 1973).
12. John Kelly, "Criminal Libel and Free Speech" (1958) 6 *Kansas Law Review* 295, 301 citing 8 *Holdsworth, History of English Law* (2d ed 1937) 336.
13. 376 US 254 (1964).
14. 379 US 64 (1964) ("*Garrison*").
15. 379 US 64, 69 (1964), citing Thomas Emerson, "Toward a General Theory of the First Amendment", *Yale Law Journal* 72 (1963): 877, 924.
16. *Garrison,* 379 US 64, 70–76 (1964).
17. *Parmeleee v. O'Neel,* 145 Wash App 223, 186 P 3d 1094 (Ct App Wash 2008).
18. The legal argument for not allowing truth as a defence if the statement was published with a bad motive is discussed at length in Thomas Starkie,

A Treatise on the Law of Slander, Libel, Scandalum Magnatum, and False Rumors, 360–365 in reprint, 497–504 in original.
19. *Parmelee v. O'Neel*, 145 Wash App 223, 236, 186 P 3d 1094, 1100 (Ct App Wash 2008)..
20. Gideon Newmark, "The Strong Medicine of Overbreadth as Applied to Criminal Libel", *Case Western Reserve Law Review* 59 (2008–2009): 553, 568–569.
21. *Garrison*, 379 US 64, 70 fn 7 (1964).
22. *State v. Powell,* 114 NM 395, 839 P2d 139 (1992). The New Mexico Court limited the continuing validity of the statute to cases not involving public matters where actual malice was not required by *Garrison.* See Comment, "First Amendment–Criminal Libel Statute Held Unconstitutional as Applied to Public Statements Involving Public Concerns: *State v. Powell*", *New Mexico Law Review* 24 (1994): 495.
23. See, for example, *Oklahoma Statutes* 21-774.
24. David Pritchard, "Rethinking Criminal Libel: An Empirical Study", *Communication Law & Policy* 14 (2009): 303, 317, Table 3.
25. *Wisconsin Statutes* 942.01 (3) (2007–2008).
26. *State v. Baron*, 318 Wis2d 60, 86 fn 15, 760 NW2d 34, 47 (2009).
27. *Wisconsin Statutes* 942.03 (2007–2008).
28. Patrick Milmo and W. Rogers (eds), *Gatley on Libel and Slander*, 771.
29. Ibid.
30. Geoffrey Robertson and Andrew Nicol, *Robertson & Nicol on Media Law*, 266–284.
31. Larry Eldridge, *A Distant Heritage—The Growth of Free Speech in Early America*. For a general discussion of free speech in colonial America, see Leonard Levy, *Freedom of Speech and Press in Early American History: Legacy of Suppression*, 18–87.
32. Norman Rosenberg, *Protecting the Best Men: An Interpretive History of the Law of Libel*, 17.
33. Eldridge, 91–97. Similar types of punishment were utilised in contemporary England. Gregory Lisby, "No Place in the Law: The Ignominy of Criminal Libel in American Jurisprudence", *Communication Law & Policy* 9 (2004): 433, 448.
34. Eldridge, 97.
35. Ibid., 117.
36. Ibid., 1024–1025.
37. See Pritchard, 313–314.

38. Media Law Resource Center, "Criminal Libel Update" (Dec. 2009) *MLRC Bulletin* 123, 171–172.
39. Lisby, 434–435.
40. *Ashton v. Kentucky*, 384 US 195, 198 (1966).
41. Pritchard, 316.
42. Ibid., 317.
43. Ibid.
44. 47 *USC* Sec 230(c).
45. Section 230(c) overturns a contrary trial court holding in *Stratton Oakmont v. Prodigy Services Co*, 23 Media L Rptr 1794 (New York Supreme Ct 1995).
46. Newmark, 560.
47. Walker, 203.
48. See generally, Pritchard, 318–338.
49. *Mink v. Knox*, 613 F.3d 995 (10th Cir. 2010).
50. Case 1:04-cv-00023-LTB, Slip Opinion, USDC Colorado, filed June 3, 2011, p. 13.
51. Jon Ingold, "Free Speech Suit Settled in 'Howling Pig' Case, *denverpost.com*, retrieved at www.denverpost.com/fdcp?unique=1323801399977.
52. 379 US 64, 69 (1964).
53. Milmo and Rogers, 794.
54. Milmo and Rogers, 795. See Walker, 177.
55. Milmo and Rogers, 774. See Jeremy Feigelson and Erik Bierbauer, "Criminal Defamation: International Reforms Advance Against a Global Danger" (2002) 2 *Libel Defense Resource Center Bulletin* 107, 117.
56. *Coroners and Justice Act (2009)* (UK) 73(b) (effective 12 January 2010).
57. Clare Ovey and Robin White, *Jacobs & White, The European Convention on Human Rights*, 328.
58. *Cumpana v. Romania*, decision of Grand Chamber, European Court of Human Rights, Appeal 33348/96 (17 December 2004) paragraphs 25-37; retrieved at: http://cmiskp.echr.coe.int/tkp197/view.asp?action = html& documentId = 709499&portal = hbkm&source = externalbydocnumber& table = F69A27FD8FB86142BF01C1166DEA398649.
59. Ibid., paragraph 116.
60. Ibid., paragraph 119. The Euro 2033 fine was not disturbed.
61. Elena Yanchukova, "Criminal defamation and Insult Laws: An Infringement on the Freedom of Expression in European and Post-Communist

Jurisdictions", *Columbia Journal of Transnational Law* 41 (2003): 861, 871–875.

62. *American Convention on Human Rights,* adopted by the Organisation of American States 22 November 1969, entered into force 18 July 1978 (*American Convention*). See Liam Gearon, *Freedom of Expression and Human Rights*, 165. The *American Convention* has been ratified by twenty-four of the member States of the Organization of American States. The United States, however, is not a signatory. While Venezuela is a signatory, its continued adherence to the *American Convention* may be problematic.
63. The jurisdiction of the Inter-American Court and the Inter-American Commission on Human Rights to hear disputes is discussed in Jo Pasqualucci, "Criminal defamation and the Evolution of the Doctrine of Freedom of Expression in International Law: Comparative Jurisprudence of the Inter-American Court of Human Rights", *Vanderbilt Journal of Transnational Law* 39 (2006): 379, 384–386.
64. Ibid., 403.
65. See *Defamation Act* 2005 (NSW) Sec 5. Under the NSW statute, the prosecution must prove that the defendant knew that the defamatory statements were false.
66. Walker, 194. Professor Walker's article provides a survey of the status of criminal libel among common law jurisdictions, pp. 193–195.
67. Leflar, 1028–1034; Lisby, 438.
68. Lisby, 438.
69. Emile Durkheim, *The Division of Labor in Society,* W. Halls trans, 44; Anthony Giddens: *Emile Durkheim, Selected Writings*, Anthony Giddens trans, 124.

Chapter 4

The Origins of Civilisation

Durkheim versus Marx

Of the three most well-known classical social theorists—Karl Marx, Emile Durkheim, and Max Weber—Durkheim has not traditionally fared as well as the other two among modern thinkers, in part, because of his innate conservatism.[1] But that does not mean that he was wrong. In fact, there is a substantial overlap between Durkheim and twentieth-century theorist Jurgen Habermas who began his career influenced by Marx. This chapter offers further support for the continued vitality and validity of Durkheim's theories. Whereas the discussion in the preceding chapter of the demise of criminal defamation, as explained by the division of labour and the rise of organic solidarity, offers direct evidence of the validity of Durkheim's sociology in the context of freedom of expression, the discussion in this chapter is more general. By examining modern archaeological evidence, the argument will be made that Durkheim's concept of social evolution was correct. The story's antagonists are Karl Marx and his followers.

Marx was not just a social theorist but also a political revolutionary whereas Durkheim was unimpressed with politics and politicians and was adamant that the sociologist should solely occupy the role of observer and not that of changer of society. By the same token, with the fall of communism, Marx's theories have certainly fallen from favour with respect to politics. However, in certain areas, Marxist thought still appears to have a significant influence and the time has come to re-evaluate some Marxist theory in the light of Durkheim's so-called conservative approach. One area where Marxist thought appears to have dominated scholarship for at least fifty years is the theory of the origins of civilisation employed by anthropologists. As it now develops, there is valid reason based on archaeology to question Marxist theory and reconsider alternatives offered by Durkheim.

Durkheim was singularly unimpressed with Marx and concluded that Marx's dogma of economic materialism was seriously deficient and reflected basic misunderstandings of social life. Most specifically, Durkheim believed that religion, as opposed to economics, was the most basic social phenomenon and that everything in society such as law, morality, politics, and science can be traced back to religion. Durkheim argued that economics was not the source of these societal traits but that economics was a circumstance derived from religion.[2] Weber, in contrast, ultimately had the safest argument among the three because he maintained that it was naïve and counterproductive to try to reduce social transformations to a single cause.[3] Durkheim ultimately concluded that the secondary influence of economics on society required the conclusion that the growth of large-scale capitalist enterprises did not require the overthrow of the existing social order and that Marxist theory was simply incorrect and theoretically unsound.[4] Fundamentally, Marx believed that religion was a mechanism that justified the existing social order to satisfy the needs of the population. In other words, religion supported the existing class order and its inequities. Durkheim, while not a particularly religious man personally, is not as dismissive of religion as a constructive force and argued that religion must reflect "profound truths about the relationship between society and its members."[5]

Durkheim's divergence from Marxist thought is perhaps nowhere as pronounced as with respect to the theory of civilisation. While theory of civilisation is a relatively modern concept, Marxist thinking has played a major role among anthropologists. Civilisation is a term used by anthropologists to refer to a culture that has attained a certain level of development. There have been numerous definitions used by anthropologists to distinguish civilisations from more basic or less complex cultural progenitors. The definitions are generally in accord with Durkheim's view of the transition from mechanical to organic solidarity. Civilisation is very much akin to urbanisation as the definitions have a great deal in common. V. Gordon Childe described a civilised society as one which displayed the following criteria:

1. Increase in settlement size toward urban proportions;
2. Centralised accumulation of capital resulting from the imposition of tribute or taxation;
3. Monumental public works;
4. The invention of writing;
5. Advances toward exact and predictive sciences;
6. The appearance and growth of long-distance trade in luxuries;
7. The emergence of a class-stratified society;
8. The freeing of a part of the population from subsistence tasks for full-time craft specialisation;
9. The substitution of a politically organized society based on territorial principles, the state, for one based on kin ties; and
10. The appearance of naturalistic, or perhaps better, representational art.[6]

Anthropologist Robert Adams described civilisation as a society with interrelated institutions:

1. Class stratification marked by highly different degrees of ownership of control of the main productive resources;

2. Political and religious hierarchies complementing each other in the administration of territorially organised states; and
3. Complex division of labour with full-time craftsmen, servants, soldiers and officials alongside the great mass of primary peasant works.[7]

Professor Clyde Kluckhohn distilled the nature of civilisation as cultural groups that exhibited at least two of these three qualities: towns with populations exceeding five thousand, a written language, and monumental ceremonial centres.[8] Based on these and similar definitions, highly respected archaeologist Glyn Daniel identified indigenous civilisations of antiquity as including: Mesopotamia (Sumer), Egypt, Indus Valley, Yellow River China, Inca, Aztec, and the Maya.[9] While these are not the only indigenous civilisations, they are believed to be the oldest. By indigenous, it is meant that by and large, they grew outside the orbit of existing civilisations. Civilisation, under any of the definitions, clearly involves urbanisation, specialisation, and an ability to support a concentrated population which, in turn, requires agriculture. It is not difficult to take this one step further and define civilisation as the transition from mechanical to organic solidarity, and indeed Professor Martin Singer has proffered exactly that analysis. In the symposium called City Invincible held at the University of Chicago in 1958, Professor Singer described civilisation in very Durkheimian terms.

Professor Singer explained that in small societies, Durkheim posited there would be little differentiation among individuals and that there would be a lack of control over the environment—mechanical solidarity. In contrast, organic solidarity found in more complex societies would be built on differentiation among the members. Singer pointed out that division of labour is a function of moral density which Durkheim defined as a function of population density or is derived from improvements in transport and communication. In the more primitive or mechanically organised society, there is effective isolation between groups. As isolation and homogeneity of the community decreases, secularisation and individuality increase, leading to organic solidarity and the opportunity for division of labour.[10] While Professor Singer's description of civilisation is certainly true to Durkheim's concepts of mechanical and organic solidarity, the description of civilisation begs the rather obvious question of why did mechanical solidarity give way to organic solidarity in the first place. Why did some cultural groups undergo the urban revolution? What propelled the development of civilisation?

It is in this area that Marxist-influenced thinking has long held sway. The procuring cause of the factors or cultural attributes that are defined as civilisation has been commonly held to be the development of agriculture. Once individuals no longer had to spend all of their time foraging for food, some individuals could become professional soldiers, others medical practitioners, merchants, and various other occupations. Given that sustenance is an essential element of existence, the theory is by no means far-fetched. But, it does elevate economics above other factors and thus the Marxist influence. The concept essentially became ingrained as established theory for generations of anthropologists primarily through the arguments of Australian anthropologist V. Gordon Childe who was a committed acolyte of Marx, Lenin, and Stalin. Indeed, in 1957, Childe eventually took his own life in the aftermath of Khrushchev's speech revealing Stalin's atrocities and the savage repression of the Hungarian uprising of 1956.[11]

In Childe's own, somewhat revisionist, final words on the subject, published in 1958 shortly after his death:

> Since "means of production" figure so conspicuously in the archaeological record, I suppose most prehistorians are inclined to be so far Marxists as to wish to assign them a determining role among the behaviour patterns they have fossilized. They can do so even in the USA without invoking the Fifth Amendment, since it was to the "mode of production" ("means" plus "relations") that Marx attributed such a dominating influence. By 1936 I had advanced beyond this in so far as I insisted on the need for concentrating the surplus to accomplish the Urban Revolution....

Childe continued:

> In the new *Dawn* of 1939 I paid lip-service to "Marxism" in a standardised scheme for the description of cultures: first the food quest, then secondary industries and trade, only thereafter social and religious institutions in so far as they can be inferred or deduced.[12]

The key sequence of events leading to civilisation according to Childe is (1) food, that is agriculture, (2) then specialised industry, and (3) finally, religious institutions to stabilise the ruling order. This theory became firmly entrenched as orthodoxy and perhaps reached its culmination in Karl Wittfogel's seminal work *Oriental Despotism—A Comparative Study of Total Power* in which the author carried agriculture one step further and argued in a work consisting of over four hundred and fifty pages of text that irrigation, or what he termed "hydraulics", is the ultimate force propelling a society into civilisation. Wittfogel's focus is on "hydraulic society" which he described as being the necessary precursor of agriculture. Wittfogel was initially also a passionate Marxist but fell out with Communist Party theoreticians over the issue of the significance of bureaucracy in ancient hydraulic societies because his position evidently deviated from Marxist orthodoxy. As a result, Wittfogel devotes many pages of his book to the defence of his argument in light of Marxist-Leninist doctrine and perceived errors made by Marx in the actual historical record of Asiatic societies.[13] In fact, it is now acknowledged that Asiatic societies did not possess the egalitarian village base predicted by Marx.[14]

Although Wittfogel had a profound and extremely hostile falling out with communism, both he and Childe maintained that the propelling force for civilisation was materialist determinism—hydraulic society in the former and, more broadly, agriculture for the latter and that is where the state of anthropological theory sat for many years. As observed by Professor Adams: "At least from the viewpoint of understanding sociocultural change, the crucial variable…is the gross amount of deployable wealth or surplus."[15] Whether or not hydraulics and agriculture are viewed as Marxist-influenced theories for societal development, both concepts are far removed from Durkheim's argument that religion is the principle propelling force in human society. Durkheim rejected economics as the fundamental driving force in societal development in a three-step unambiguous rejection of Marx.

Durkheim first recognised that Marx espoused economic materialism as the key element in historical development:

> The principle [of Marxism] states that in the last analysis historical development depends upon economic causes. This is what has been called the dogma of economic materialism.[16]

Durkheim then noted that Marx's arguments for setting economic factors as the main propellant for progress were inadequate to justify this conclusion:

> Just as it seems true to us that the causes of social phenomena must be sought outside individual representations, so does it seem false to us to bring them down in the last resort, to the state of industrial technology and to make the economic factor the mainspring of progress. Even without setting against economic materialism any definite fact, how can one fail to notice the inadequacy of the proofs on which it rests?[17]

Durkheim concluded that Marx's conclusions are in error because fundamentally all manifestations of collective activity are a function of religion, including economics:

> Not only is the Marxist hypothesis unproven, but it is contrary to facts which appear established. Sociologists and historians tend increasingly to come together in their common affirmation that religion is the most primitive of all social phenomenon. It is from it that have emerged, through successive transformations, all the other manifestations of collective activity, law, morality, art, science, political forms, etc. In principle, everything is religious. Yet we know of no means of reducing religion to economics nor of any attempt at really effecting this reduction... More generally, it is

> beyond dispute that, at the origin, the economics factor is rudimentary, while, by contrast, religious life is rich and pervasive. How therefore could the latter result from the former and, on the contrary, is it not probable that the economy depends on religion rather than vice versa?[18]

Childe maintained that civilisation follows the progression: agriculture (Wittfogel argued hydraulics), then specialisation of labour, followed third by religion, while Durkheim would clearly put religion ahead of economics as a propellant for social change. Could the answer as to who was correct be found in the archaeological record of early civilisations?

Following Childe's theory, sometimes viewed as virtually a law of anthropology, social scientists assumed that organised religion emerged as a mechanism for maintaining the social order or class structure of urban societies that were based on agriculture (hydraulics).[19] Until relatively recently, it was difficult to dispute this concept based on physical evidence because it is difficult to accurately date the relative emergence of agriculture, human specialisation, and religious institutions at a specific archaeological site. However, based on recent excavations in Turkey, there is newly discovered evidence that supports the argument that the development of agriculture may have been subsequent to the development of monumental ritual and religious centres. Much of this information has been developed from excavations conducted at Catalhoyuk and Gobekli Tepe. The construction of monumental religious sites in these two locations predates the emergence of the classical indigenous civilisations discussed in Glyn Daniel's standard work, *The First Civilisations,* which places the most ancient civilisation, Sumer, at around 3200 BC, whereas Gobekli Tepe in Turkey shows clear evidence of monumental architecture dating back before 8000 BC.[20] It has even been suggested that "it seems quite possible that people who had come together largely because of large ritual centres ended up accidentally domesticating plants and animals."[21]

There are several ways to view these archaeological results. One view is that the evidence supports that organized religion precedes the development of agriculture in civilisation and that Childe was simply wrong and Durkheim was correct. However, there does not yet seem to be support for this proposition among anthropologists. A second view is that agriculture and religion are inextricably wound together in the development of urban society or civilisation. Finally, there is the third perspective that one size does not fit all and that in some civilisations, agriculture preceded religion (Childe, Wittfogel) and that in others, religious imperatives created the need for agriculture (Durkheim). Both the second and third alternatives find support among archaeologists, and both offer validity to Durkheim's social theory.

In connection with Catalhoyuk, archaeologists are virtually "unanimous" on religion contributing to the changes leading to civilisation. Several of the archaeologists chose to emphasise the causal force of the symbolic (religious) whereas anthropologist Ian Hodder argued for a mutual relationship between the materialistic and symbolic forces as the propellants toward civilisation—this is known as the "entanglement" of material and spiritual spheres.[22] Indeed, the consensus of archaeologists was more in line with the concept of entanglement:

> It came to be widely agreed among the group that picking apart causal claims was fraught with difficulties and that the most likely answer to the general question is that religious life and socioeconomic life were and are inextricably linked.[23]

However, the situation with Gobekli Tepe is somewhat less ambiguous, and there are clearer arguments for the emergence of a religious centre prior to domestication of plants.[24] As Ian Hodder has noted, Gobekli Tepe is "remarkable" and raises "the possibility of a very early role for symbolism and ritual in the formation of settled agricultural life."[25]

Gobekli Tepe is a massive site that has been described as bearing some resemblance to Stonehenge and has been dated to having been built about 11,000 years ago. Some of the stones weigh sixteen tons and had to be transported without benefit of wheels.[26] One of the primary archaeologists involved in the excavation is Klaus Schmidt. The site consists of rings of pillars on a monumental scale. But, there is no evidence of a water supply or of habitation. There is also no onsite evidence of agriculture or even cooking fires. It appears to have been purely a ceremonial centre.[27] Gobekli Tepe never developed into a civilisation because the urban centre never formed. But, under Childe's or Wittfogel's analysis, Gobekli Tepe never should have developed. Major religious centres are expected to be a product of agriculture—required to maintain class order and discipline in hydraulic society. In Schmidt's analysis, Gobekli Tepe demonstrated a reversal of Childe's hypothesis. Namely, organised religion came before the emergence of agriculture and specialisation. Incredibly, the monumental construction was initially supported by foragers and that cultivation of grains emerged later in a nearby site to support workers and worshippers.[28]

Perhaps rather imaginatively or wistfully, Gobekli Tepe has been described as a Neolithic Disneyland with accommodations and dining emerging around the centre as a consequence of the existence of the centre and that agriculture was developed to serve the needs of travellers who came to participate in ritual.[29] While no consensus has formed concerning Gobekli Tepe, it certainly can support a thesis that civilisation can emerge through different paths. However, despite Schmidt's enthusiasm for dual paths toward civilisation, there is a weakness in the argument. Gobekli Tepe never evolved into a civilisation, which has been described as urbanisation or the urban revolution. While agriculture eventually developed, there is no historical record of habitation. Consequently, the argument might be made that while organised religion may precede agriculture, it is only in societies where agriculture precedes organised religion that civilisation ultimately emerges. In this light, the dual paths to civilisation have yet to be proven. More realistically, Hodder's concept of inextricable entanglement between religion and agriculture seems more viable and safer.

While Marxist influenced ideas continue to have a significant presence in theory concerning the emergence of civilisation, ongoing excavations in Turkey have cast substantial doubt on the correctness of this influence. Gordon Childe and Karl Wittfogel wrote with such authority that their arguments were accepted without thorough archaeological verification. In light of new evidence, it is clearly incorrect to write off Durkheim's thoughts concerning the limitations of materialism as applied to the emergence of civilisation. Durkheim was quite adamant that theory must be supported by empirical evidence. The winds of change are perhaps in the air, and it is at least necessary to recognise that spirituality as well as materialism was a significant and transformative factor in the evolution from mechanical to organic solidarity or from hunter-gather to civilised existence.

ENDNOTES

1. John Hughes, Wes Sharrock and Peter Martin, *Understanding Classical Sociology*, 2003: 145, 201.
2. Emile Durkheim, "The Materialist Conception of History", *Revue Philosophique* 44 (1897): 645–651, translated in Emile Durkheim, *The Rules of the Sociological Method and Selected Texts on Sociology and Its Method* (Steven Lukes ed, W. Halls trans), 167–174 and Anthony Giddens, *Emile Durkheim: Selected Writings*, 159–162 (This article was Durkheim's review of Antonio Labriola's book concerning historical materialism). See generally Emile Durkheim, *The Elementary Forms of Religious Life* (Joseph Swain trans.).
3. See Dragan Milovanovic, *An Introduction to the Sociology of Law*, 45–47.
4. Durkheim, *The Rules of the Sociological Method*, 174.
5. Hughes, 180.
6. Robert Adams, *The Evolution of Urban Society–Early Mesopotamia and Prehispanic Mexico*, 10.
7. Glyn Daniel, *The First Civilisations—The Archeology of Their Origins*, 13.
8. Ibid., 12.
9. Ibid., 9–10.
10. Milton Singer, "The Expansion of Society and Its Cultural Implications" in Carl Kraeling and Robert Adams (eds), *City Invincible*, 252.
11. Indeed, Childe remains a darling of the socialists and communists. See Neil Faulkner, 'Gordon Childe and Marxist Archeology' (2007) 116 *International Socialism*, retrieved at www.isj.org.uk/index.php4?id=367=116.
12. V. Gordon Childe in Glyn Daniel and Christopher Chippindale (eds), *The Pastmasters—Eleven Modern Pioneers of Archeology*, 16.
13. Karl Wittfogel, *Oriental Despotism—A Comparative Study of Total Power*, 1–10, 369–412.
14. Bruce Trigger, *Understanding Early Civilisations—A Comparative Study*, 52.
15. Adams, 46.
16. Durkheim, *The Rules of the Sociological Method*, 167.
17. Ibid., 172.
18. Ibid., 173.

19. Charles Mann, “Birth of Religion”, *National Geographic* 219 (2011): 34, 56.
20. Ian Hodder (ed), *Religion in the Emergence of Civilisation: Catalhoyuk As a Case Study*, 18.
21. Ibid.
22. LeRon Shults, “Spiritual Entanglement: Transforming Religious Symbols at Catalhoyuk” in Hodder, 92.
23. Ian Hodder, “Conclusions and Evaluation” in Hodder, 339.
24. For a discussion of some of the excavations in detail, see Joris Peters and Klaus Schmidt, “Animals in the Symbolic World of Pre-Pottery Neolithic Gobekli Tepe, South-Eastern Turkey: A Preliminary Assessment”, *Anthropozoologica* 39 (2004): 179.
25. Hodder, 339.
26. Mann, 39.
27. Ibid., 42.
28. Ibid., 57.
29. Ibid.

Chapter 5

Traditional, Philosophical, and Legal Views

A Tour of Free Speech Theory

In chapter 2, justifications for free speech based on division of labour in society were discussed independently of more traditional free speech theories. In this chapter, traditional free speech theory will be presented in a similar stand-alone type of argument. In the following chapter, the two approaches will be compared, distinguished and harmonised with the goal of creating a balanced approach to free speech and the competing interests. In chapter 7, the appropriateness of raising sociological argument in the context of First Amendment interpretation is discussed. But, for now, there is a paradigm shift away from Emile Durkheim and Jurgen Habermas and toward John Stuart Mill and Immanuel Kant. Initially, American readers should appreciate that freedom of expression is not by any means identical with the First Amendment even though a great deal of freedom of expression arguments have been couched in First Amendment terms. The First Amendment is part of the Constitution of the United States and is a legal rather than philosophical or sociological concept. However, in common parlance, especially among American scholars, the First Amendment is frequently treated as if it were synonymous, or at least the legal equivalent, with freedom of expression itself. While arguments for freedom of expression extend to speech considerably exterior to recognised First Amendment rights, in keeping with American convention, First Amendment and freedom of expression will be used interchangeably in this discussion with the understanding that actual freedom of speech is a broader concept.

There is a constantly growing body of literature concerning free speech, and any attempt at organised discussion requires that the various arguments and theories be organised in some type of taxonomy. As discussed in chapter 1, current scholarship maintains there are two justifications for free speech: the instrumental justification and the constitutive justification. The classic reasons for free speech may also be called positive reasons for free speech as opposed to a negative reason such as Professor Schauer's argument concerning American distrust of government. This theory suggests that any form of regulation is inherently suspect because of the general tendency of governments to over-regulate or suppress speech.[1] The instrumental/constitutive dichotomy is comprehensive because all of the efficacious or results-oriented reasons for free speech are defined as instrumental with the moral residue falling within the constitutive justification. As defined by Professor Dworkin, the instrumental justification for free speech is that—although there may not be an inherent moral right to freedom of speech—free speech is desirable because it will help to attain desirable benefits, usually political, for the public at large.[2] Free speech assists in the achievement of specific goals. Conversely, constitutive justification holds that freedom of speech is valuable not as an instrument to help create a better society but because freedom of speech is an essential constituent part of a just society and is an essential part of human dignity.[3] Constitutive justification perhaps can be distilled as meaning that free speech is intrinsically a good and moral thing without regard to how well it helps to achieve specific goals such as democracy or, as it is also called, self-government. This justification accommodates the more visceral response that free speech is good because we like it or that it makes us feel good.

Although commonly employed, there are, nevertheless, limitations in describing free speech justifications as either instrumental or constitutive because the resulting categorisations are inevitably somewhat contrived and artificial and are not always satisfactory in that many of the arguments do not fit within precise categories and, in any event, overlap with each other. Nevertheless, this approach is useful simply because of the volume of material that must be considered. The two broad justifications for free speech are, in turn, supported by theories. For example, John Stuart Mill's seminal truth theory is the progenitor of numerous other theories, including the democracy theory and the marketplace of ideas theory. Together these theories fit within the instrumental justification. Immanuel Kant's philosophy of individual autonomy and the supporting theory of self-realisation are closely related and provide theoretical support for the constitutive justification for free speech.

Another but less well-known approach for categorising the different free speech theories or ideas was discussed by David Tucker who, like Dworkin, found two baskets in which to place the theories. Tucker elected to utilise two recognised and distinctive principles of moral philosophy—functional and deontological.[4] Functionalism is a utilitarian or consequential perspective and would include the instrumental justification, which, in turn, includes much of John Stuart Mill's truth theory as well as Alexander Meiklejohn's democracy theory. The deontological perspective "focuses on the inherent rightness or wrongness of particular actions, regardless of the consequences those actions might produce."[5] In other words, free speech is simply a good thing regardless of what it may or may not lead to. The deontological perspective to free speech perhaps finds its clearest exponent in Kant's belief in autonomy. Similar to Dworkin, Tucker makes the point that the functional reasons, like the instrumental justification, are generally geared toward reasons that speak in terms of consequences and tangible results while the deontological reasons are more deeply rooted in Kant's deeply anti-consequentialist philosophy of autonomy or, in traditional parlance, the constitutive justification.

While there have been attempts from time to time to present a single unified theory of free speech, these attempts have been largely unsuccessful for a number of reasons including the absence of support from other scholars or courts.[6] For example, the noted First Amendment scholar, Thomas Emerson, articulated a unified theory of freedom of speech that attempted to include all of the reasons relating to free speech within what has become known as the expression-action theory.[7] Under this theory, "expression" was protected whereas "action" did not receive First Amendment protection. By way of example, screaming about corrupt politicians would fall within the rubric of protected expression whereas shooting corrupt politicians would not be entitled to protection as falling within the category of action.

However, Emerson's theory presented problems because some of the conclusions seemed to require somewhat strained reasoning. For example, defamatory speech on political matters was protected as expression but defamatory speech directed towards individuals was not protected because it constituted action, the action being the hurt feelings of the person being defamed.[8] Unfortunately, this type of distinction tended to undermine the theory because it would appear as if the theory were being contorted to accommodate a result rather than being genuinely predictive. In other words, if you did not know that private libels were actionable in the United States, the expression-action theory would seem to predict naturally that such behaviour constitutes expression and is therefore protected activity. It is only with the knowledge of the real-world result that the theory is manipulated to lead to the correct result.

THE MAJOR REASONS AND THEORIES SUPPORTING FREE SPEECH

In addition to the conceptually based instrumental/constitutive system for categorising free speech theories, there is also an approach that is more descriptive. Professors Thomas Tedford and Dale Herbeck discuss free speech in terms of three reasons or rationales.[9] These rationales include philosophical, political, and individual reasons for freedom of expression:

> [T]he philosophical (free speech is vital to the search for truth), the political (free speech is necessary to political liberty and democratic self-government), and the individual (free speech is essential to human dignity and personal self-fulfilment).[10]

A possible advantage of employing this three-part analysis is that it is simply clearer than employing terms such as instrumental, constitutive, functional, and deontological. That is, the three-part categorisation looks at the theories on their face rather than categorising them using a theoretical rubric based on the type of result ultimately attained. Simply for structural purposes, this discussion will adopt a modified form of the organisation employed by Tedford and Herbeck and the various theories will be considered under the general categories of philosophical, political, and individual, with the understanding that the first two reasons are inherently instrumental while the third is usually a constitutive justification. As will become apparent, the instrumental theories overlap and ultimately, it is suggested that the instrumental theories are all, in varying degrees, derivative of John Stuart Mill's argument that free speech is desirable because it leads to the discovery of truth.

A. The Philosophical Reason

Perhaps the most cited and well-known philosophical argument in favour of free speech appears in the mid-nineteenth century writings of John Stuart Mill.[11] Fundamentally, Mill maintained that free and open discussion was essential to the ultimate discovery of the truth.[12] Mill's theory has also been described as the "best perspectives or solutions" theory.[13] The premise is that the absence of restraints on speech will facilitate discovery of the truth.[14] In more contemporary parlance, the truth theory was restated by US Supreme Court Justice Oliver Wendell Holmes in terms of the marketplace of ideas.[15] Mill apparently derived his theory from John Milton's *Areopagitica: A Speech for the Liberty of Unlicensed*

Printing that appeared in 1644. The truth and marketplace of ideas theories have been very influential in the development of all free speech theory. Before discussing Mill and Holmes in detail, some of the earlier arguments that support their theories bear examination.

Historical Antecedents of the Philosophy Based Theories

While there are antecedents in ancient Athens and republican Rome, the modern concept of free speech perhaps finds clearer roots in the Protestant Reformation.[16] Martin Luther, in the sixteenth century, openly dissented from the teachings of the Catholic Church in an era when such views were punishable by death. The very act of preaching in defiance of established authority, even though confined within the sphere of religion, was nothing less than a statement that the individual had a right to take a verbal stand against accepted authority. In the seventeenth century, John Milton, a Puritan philosopher and poet, became involved in free speech in response to the ability of the Crown to censor publications through licensing laws. However, Milton's concern was not with punishment after publication but rather with prepublication censorship, now referred to as prior restraint. [17] The rejection of prior restraint means that "publishing will be treated like most other activities of which the law takes notice" and legal repercussions follow commission of the tort.[18] In Milton's time, all books had to be approved by the Church of England prior to publication and only certain printers were permitted to publish books. The result, of course, was censorship. In his *Areopagitica,* Milton argued the case for unlicensed printing so that he could enjoy "the liberty to know, to utter and to argue freely according to conscience."[19] However, since Milton's writings were suppressed upon the restoration of the Monarchy in the late seventeenth century, the immediate impact of the *Areopagitica* was limited.[20]

Milton's seventeenth-century arguments that freedom of speech contributed to knowledge certainly presaged John Stuart Mill's formal elucidation of the truth theory in the mid-nineteenth century. But, a later seventeenth-century philosopher, Benedict de Spinoza, seems to have anticipated the twentieth-century revisions to Mill's theory. Spinoza, much like some of the twentieth-century philosophers, recognised that the discovery of truth was not the inevitable outcome from freedom of expression because truth was not an absolute and was itself subject to change. To Spinoza, the value of freedom of expression lay in the process of debate and exchange of ideas rather than in some idealised concept of discovering the truth. Spinoza valued discussion and the thinking process reflected by discussion.[21] Bearing elements of instrumental results-oriented reasoning coupled with a somewhat Kantian belief in the virtue of the existence of free speech as a liberating force creating a better person, more so than other pre- twentieth-century free speech theorists, Spinoza's perspective was a combination of instrumental and constitutive justifications. Despite Spinoza's sophisticated reasoning and its likely attractiveness to twenty-first-century readers, it was another Englishman, following in the footsteps of Milton, who moved free speech along the path that led to modern doctrinal law.

While Milton laid the groundwork for the theory that truth emerges from free speech, it was John Locke who articulated revolutionary arguments that were not lost on his American cousins. Locke did not, however, espouse an unlimited freedom of speech as his toleration for different religious views was limited; but, an absolutist argument for free speech was articulated at about the same time by the French philosopher Pierre Bayle. While Thomas Jefferson apparently possessed an English translation of Bayle's leading work in his library, it is unknown whether James Madison, the author of the American Bill of Rights, was aware of the book or its contents.[22]

In the late seventeenth century, Locke advocated that there should be a degree of religious toleration, that government existed by the consent of the governed, and that the governed retained a right to revolution.[23] Following close on the heels of Locke's ideas, the eighteenth century produced a substantial amount of free speech discussion in the political sphere. The *United States Declaration of Independence,* written in 1776 and drafted primarily by Jefferson, in the second paragraph, specifically references that governments derive their powers "from the consent of the governed," and that whenever a government fails in its responsibilities, "it is the right of the people to alter or to abolish it." The concept of public sovereignty cannot be separated from the right of free speech because free speech is the mechanism by which the people exercise their dominion over government.[24] In support of the relationship between liberty and freedom of speech, Englishmen Thomas Gordon and John Trenchard wrote an essay in the early eighteenth century entitled *On Freedom of Speech* in which they said:

> There can be no such thing as public liberty without freedom of speech, which is the right of every man, as far as by it he does not hurt and control the right of another. This is the only check which it ought to suffer, the only bounds which it ought to know.[25]

Gordon and Trenchard seem to have anticipated the ongoing tension among privacy, defamation law, and freedom of speech.

Just two years before the *Declaration of Independence* (1776), English legal scholar James Burgh wrote that freedom of speech relating to government officials should be unhindered and not subject to the laws of defamation for fear of deterring criticism.[26] Subsequent to Burgh, but still a half century before Mill, the American revolutionary Thomas Paine, in the dedication page of a controversial tract that was highly critical of organised religions, anticipated Mill's arguments:

> I have always strenuously supported the right of every man to his own opinion, however different that opinion might be to mine. He who denies to another this right, makes a slave of himself to his present opinion, because he precludes himself the right of changing it. The most formidable weapon against errors of every kind is reason.[27]

Paine concluded with logic that is virtually identical to the later words of Mill: "when opinions are free, either in matters of government or religion, truth will finally and powerfully prevail."[28]

The Truth Theory

In the mid-nineteenth century, the philosopher John Stuart Mill articulated comprehensive theoretical arguments for free speech. It is important to note, however, that Mill as well as his predecessors primarily focused on freedom of speech with respect to ideas or opinions rather than facts. The concept of permitting freedom of speech with respect to factual statements evolved slowly and cannot be definitively attributed to a single source. This evolution from opinion to fact is also complicated because the legal distinction between fact and opinion is not altogether clear. In modern defamation law, ostensible statements of opinion may be treated more like factual statements if the opinion is contingent on underlying assumptions (facts) that are capable of being objectively ascertained as true or false.

In 1859, Mill's seminal work, *On Liberty*, was published and, in this book, Mill argued that individual freedom must be paramount except in cases where the act of the individual impairs the rights of others. Mill believed the "the only part of the conduct of anyone for which he is amenable to society, is that which concerns others."[29] He also maintained that liberty of expression was even more important than speaking the truth. Mill theorised that when truth encountered falsehood, truth would inevitably emerge victorious. It is also quite clear that Mill had substantial fear of the repression that could be inflicted by a majoritarian democracy.[30] Ultimately, Mill's arguments for freedom of speech can be distilled into four related points:

- If the speech that is suppressed contains the truth, then truth itself is suppressed.
- Since the permitted speech and the suppressed speech may each contain elements of truth and falsity, it is only through advocacy of both positions that the ultimate truth can be ascertained.
- If the permitted speech contains the absolute truth and all of the suppressed speech is false, the truth is still imperilled because it cannot be tested against alternative hypotheses and turns into something less than proven fact.

- Ideas which cannot be challenged tend to devolve into prejudice more than fact and ultimately lose their vitality.[31]

Mill recognised that speech lost its protected status when it amounted to instigation of harmful activity. So, a matter which is expressed as ethical conviction would invariably be protected whereas actual instigation of wrongful activity, such as a lynching, would have lost its protected status.[32] Underlying all of Mill's points is the idea that freedom of speech will ultimately move in the direction of determining the truth. While this thinking has been universally regarded as a significant contribution to free speech theory, it has also generated a substantial amount of criticism. This criticism will be considered together with responses to the related marketplace of ideas theory.

The Marketplace of Ideas Theory

In the first half of the twentieth century, US Supreme Court Justices Oliver Wendell Holmes and Louis Brandeis adapted Mill's theory into more contemporary language and spoke in terms that free speech was desirable because it fostered a marketplace of ideas.[33] This very well-known presentation clearly falls within the concept of instrumental free speech because the marketplace of ideas was intended to lead to good choices and sound decisions being made by individuals and society as a whole. The Holmes/ Brandeis formulation is not so much a new theory as a new expression or rationale as to why free speech will lead to discovery of the truth.[34] In his dissent in *Abrams v. US,* Justice Holmes, joined by Justice Brandeis, objected to the majority decision upholding a criminal conviction for seditious libel.[35] In a very real sense, Holmes converted Mill's political theory into legal doctrine in his famous dissent:[36]

> But when men have realised that time has upset many fighting faiths, they may come to believe even more than they believe the very foundations of their own conduct that the ultimate good desired is better reached by free trade in ideas, that the best test of truth is the power of the thought to get itself accepted in the

> competition of the market.... That at any rate is the theory of our Constitution. It is an experiment, as all life is an experiment.[37]

Subsequently, in *Gitlow v. New York,* Holmes persuaded an extremely conservative Supreme Court to make freedom of speech as guaranteed by the First Amendment applicable to the States as well as the federal government.[38] Holmes made the then-ingenious argument that the Fourteenth Amendment's guarantee that no State would deprive citizens of life, liberty, or property without due process of law should apply to the rights guaranteed by the First Amendment. The adoption of this novel idea ultimately became a mainstay in twentieth-century Supreme Court jurisprudence and without this interpretation of the Fourteenth Amendment, the Supreme Court would not have had jurisdiction in the seminal defamation case of *New York Times Co v. Sullivan.*[39] From a jurisdictional standpoint, the *Gitlow* decision is at least as significant as *New York Times.* In the case of suppression of speech likely to lead to violence, Justice Holmes concluded that free expression of ideas must be tolerated unless the ideas presented a clear and present danger to society. However, this limitation was eventually found to be difficult to apply and ultimately the Supreme Court reformulated the test so that speech inciting violence could be suppressed only if it was intended to and likely to result in imminent lawless action.[40]

Responses to the Truth and Marketplace of Ideas Theories

Mill's truth theory, as well as Holmes' marketplace of ideas update of the truth theory, has attracted a significant amount of critical attention both supportive and unfavourable. The criticisms tend to focus on the concept of truth. First, there may be numerous situations where each opinion is equally valid and there is no objective truth. Second, Mill assumed that freedom of discussion will ultimately yield the truth or "better individual or social decisions."[41] This conclusion would seem somewhat hazardous and perhaps unwarranted. Third, Mill seemed to assume that if speech is free, then all points of view will have equal access to listeners. This is clearly incorrect as well-funded or powerful proponents may be able to drown out their opposition regardless of the merits of the opposition's point of view.

One of the leading contemporary First Amendment and free speech scholars, Frederick Schauer, offered a summary of this criticism and begins with the query: "Is the marketplace of ideas more likely to lead to knowledge than to error, ignorance, folly or nonsense?"[42] In his critique, Schauer's arguments can be paraphrased in the following way:

- The open exchange of ideas is not so much a means of ascertaining the truth as it is a means of ascertaining a consensus of opinion. It is not a test of truth but is rather a process for reaching a consensus.
- To equate truth with consensus or majority viewpoint in fact has very little to do with the truth at all.
- It does not follow as a matter of logic or reality that truth will be accepted and falsehood rejected when both are heard.
- False views may be accepted by the public who will then act in accordance with those false views with catastrophic consequences such as violence to persons or property.
- The fundamental weakness with the truth theory is that it was a product of great minds of the Enlightenment such as Mill and Jefferson who sincerely believed that reason would always prevail over emotion and prejudice.[43]

More recently, the journalist, Robert Hargreaves has made a similar criticism and concluded that decisions derived from the marketplace of ideas are "just as likely to lead to error, ignorance, folly or even to unspeakable crimes" and there is no connection "between the right to free speech and an increase in human knowledge."[44] In light of these criticisms, Mill's reasoning continues to be respected but is no longer accepted as unerringly correct.[45] For example, writing during the highly charged environment of World War II, American scholar Zechariah Chaffee, Jr. acknowledged that propaganda of all kinds interfered with reason in what he termed "friction" or a "drag on the progress of truth," but he also concluded that free speech was still the best route to discovery of the truth.[46]

Despite the criticisms, Professor Schauer is by no means dismissive of the truth theory and has added the thought that the marketplace of ideas is theoretically similar to the common law concept of cross-examination.[47] The disparate ideas compete against one another and challenge one another, much as conflicting evidence stands in contradiction in a trial. Or, conflicting ideas are comparable to the arguments made by advocates, each providing a different interpretation and meaning to the same facts, it being thought that the judge or jury, when presented with all the conflicting facts and evidence will arrive at the correct decision.[48] In this respect, if the ultimate decisions are not being made directly by the public but by less emotional and more rational decision-makers, then the multiplicity of viewpoints generated by free speech may better inform the decision makers of the various options available and lead to the discovery of the sounder viewpoint.[49] This would seem to indicate that the marketplace of ideas functions optimally when the consumers of the ideas are particularly knowledgeable and open-minded. John Stuart Mill might respond that it is the very opportunity for public debate that raises the sophistication of the public and elevates the quality of their decision-making process.

It may also be the case that if the marketplace of ideas operates as a free market, then it is probably no more efficient than any other so-called free market and suffers from the same infirmities. The marketplace may be controlled by the rich and powerful, and those individuals may manipulate the market and even deny access to the market to those who disagree with them. Through the concentration of ownership of the media and the close relationship of the media with both the financial and political communities, the marketplace of ideas might even operate more like a monolithic military-industrial complex with the controlling parties simply too closely affiliated to be able to perform their functions effectively.[50] In response to this possible shortcoming in Mill's classic truth theory, there exist various methods of guaranteeing all viewpoints equal time to respond.[51]

Another variation of the marketplace of ideas paradigm is the concept that freedom of speech provides a desirable mechanism for dissent. The First Amendment provides a vehicle whereby someone outside of the mainstream can express a minority or even unpopular viewpoint and provides "a political tilt against the powerful."[52] This concept of dissent is harmonious with American doctrinal law. While the marketplace may not— on its own—promote free speech, the constitutional protection for defamatory speech directed against public persons does, in fact, diminish the right of public officials and public figures to assert defamation claims. So, while the powerful can use free speech to promote their ideas, free speech limitations on defamation laws curtail the ability of powerful interests to restrict the free speech of others. The perspective that free speech, as a suppressant of defamation law, provides a mechanism for dissent illustrates the connection between the marketplace of ideas and the political reason for free speech.

B.The Political Reason

As an alternative to the philosophical reason that free speech is valuable because it leads to the discovery of the truth, there exists the political reason that free speech is essential to a well-functioning democratic self-government. Under the democracy or self-government theory, freedom of speech is a critical right specified in the First Amendment because it is essential for "collective self-determination" by the citizens.[53] As a general rule, speech is political when it relates to a matter under public consideration.[54] This is the clearest example of an instrumental justification because the connection between free speech and democracy is more direct than the more philosophical reason of search for truth. The political reason is supported by the democracy theory which essentially holds that free speech is essential for collective decision making and promoting citizen participation in government. In terms of free speech, the democracy theory appeals more to practical applications than the more cerebral truth theory but is nevertheless related to the truth theory. While the American scholar Alexander Meiklejohn is generally regarded as the first modern exponent of the democracy theory with respect to the First Amendment, the theory certainly has roots in the early American republic.[55]

The Democracy Theory and the Early American Republic

In 1791, ten constitutional amendments were added to the *US Constitution* that are commonly known as the Bill of Rights. These amendments had not only been contemplated at the time of the constitutional debates but it is also unlikely that the Constitution would have been ratified without the understanding that a Bill of Rights would follow.[56] James Madison was the primary draftsman of these amendments and was a major contributor to the main body of the Constitution. The First Amendment contains the words "Congress shall make no law … abridging the freedom of speech, or of the press." However straightforward those words seem on their face, their interpretation has required continuous attention by the US Supreme Court in the twentieth century, especially since 1964 when the Court decided *New York Times* and implicitly adopted the democracy theory. It is also fair to state that since the inception of the American Republic, the connection between democracy and free speech has been a recurring issue.[57]

Although free speech as a concept was formally legislated in the Bill of Rights after independence had been attained, the need for free speech concerning political affairs can be traced back to the *United States Declaration of Independence*. The second paragraph states a rather radical basis for government itself:

> We hold these truths to be self-evident, that all men are created equal, that they are endowed by their Creator with certain inalienable Rights, among these are Life, Liberty and the pursuit of Happiness. That to secure these rights, Governments are instituted among Men, deriving their just powers from the consent of the governed. That whenever any Form of Government becomes destructive of these ends, it is the right of the People to alter or to abolish it, and to institute new Government, laying its foundation on such principles

> and organizing its powers in such form, as to them shall seem most likely to effect their Safety and Happiness.[58]

This paragraph makes the argument that government is established and exists through the consent of the governed and that all authority or sovereignty is provided by the governed. If the people are sovereign and have the right to institute, alter, and abolish government, they must be accorded the same rights befitting the sovereign in any other nation-state. No one has seriously questioned the right of the sovereign to think freely and to take action accordingly. Similarly, if the sovereign is a group, that group must be able to communicate because there is no single person exercising power alone. For the group to act, the members of the group must be able to communicate. Indeed, much earlier, members of the British Parliament were granted freedom of speech within the House of Commons.

If the ultimate sovereign is neither Crown nor parliament but the people, those people must be extended the means to carry out the political process. However, if aspects of government are excluded from popular control such as selection of a monarch, then it would also follow that discussions concerning the monarch would not be justifiable under the democracy theory because extension of freedom of speech is not relevant to the ability of the people to govern. For example, under the *Constitutional Reform and Governance Act 2010 (UK)*, the Queen, Prince Charles, and Prince William now have absolute immunity from the *Freedom of Information Act 2000 (UK)*.[59] This legislation is not antidemocratic but is consistent with the democracy theory because these Royals hold office outside of the public franchise by birth right. Consequently, release of information concerning their activities does not aid in self-government but is simply disharmonious to the constitutional role of the monarchy. But, as to areas of government within popular sovereignty, it is necessary that freedom of expression and freedom of the press exist. Otherwise, the people will be unable to carry out their responsibility to institute, alter, or abolish governments. Because the majority viewpoint is not something fixed in stone but rather is subject to change, it is also essential that all viewpoints be heard because today's majority is very possibly a minority position tomorrow. Furthermore, for the majority to make up its collective mind, all viewpoints must be aired in the same way as individuals sort through ideas in their own head. Viewed as a single intellect, composed of many individuals, freedom of expression is nothing more than a traditional monarch thinking about the next step to take.

After independence had been won and the Bill of Rights enacted, the media took full advantage of the right to criticise the American government. Even venerable George Washington, on his departure from the presidency, was the subject of political cartoons that portrayed his face on the body of an ass and he was vilified in the *Aurora,* a Philadelphia newspaper:

> The man who is the source of all the misfortunes of our country, is this day reduced to a level with his fellow citizens, and is no longer possessed of power to multiply evils upon the United States. If ever there was a period for rejoicing, this is the moment...with exultation that the name of Washington from this day ceases to give currency to political iniquity, and to legalize corruption.[60]

While Washington was willing to accept this rather trenchant criticism, his immediate successor, John Adams, was not so forgiving or committed to freedom of speech in the service of democracy. At Adams' instigation, Congress enacted the *Sedition Act of 1798* that sought to outlaw criticism of government in general and of Adams in particular.[61] The congressional debates concerning the Sedition Act focused on whether the proposed law violated constitutionally guaranteed rights of free speech and, what emerged in opposition to this law were some of the clearest arguments for free speech in conduct of public affairs.[62]

Initially, the proponents of the Sedition Act insisted that the First Amendment referred only to the traditional common law prohibition of prepublication censorship known as prior restraints. Since freedom from prior restraint was only a prohibition against censorship prior to publication, the publisher still had to face whatever criminal or civil consequences the law might provide after publication.[63] In response, the opponents argued that the First Amendment had to mean more than what was already part of the common law. George Hay, a member of Congress, provided what was then the clearest articulation of the meaning of the First Amendment as a guarantee of freedom of the press. In a pamphlet, written under the pseudonym of Hortensius, he said:

> I contend therefore, that if the words freedom of the press, have any meaning at all, they mean a total exemption from any law making any publication whatever criminal....
>
> They knew that the licentiousness of the press, though an evil, was a less evil than that resulting from any law to restrain it, upon the same principle, that the most enlightened part of the world is at length convinced, that the evils arising from the toleration of heresy and atheism, are less, infinitely less, than the evils of persecution.
>
> That the spirit of inquiry and discussion, was of the utmost importance in every free country, and could be preserved only by giving it absolute protection even in its excesses.[64]

Madison also joined in the debate against the Sedition Act and wrote that the freedom guaranteed to the press by the First Amendment was absolute and that government could not be libelled.[65] However, it was not until *New York Times* was decided in 1964 that the Supreme Court definitively held that the Sedition Act was unconstitutional.

The need for freedom of speech to carry out the goals of the Declaration of Independence was noted by Alexis de Tocqueville in *Democracy in America.* De Tocqueville had the opportunity to observe and write about the young American republic and his epic work, first published in 1835, remains the most comprehensive and critical analysis of the American scene by a sympathetic though sometimes puzzled foreign observer. De Tocqueville, who might be considered a forerunner of a contemporary cultural anthropologist, concluded that "freedom of the press is a necessary consequence of the sovereignty of the people as it is understood in America:"

> In a country where the dogma of the sovereignty of the people reigns openly, censorship is not only a danger but also a great absurdity.
>
> When one accords to each a right to govern society, one must surely recognize his capacity to choose among the different opinions that agitate his contemporaries and to appreciate different facts, the knowledge of which can guide him.
>
> The sovereignty of the people and freedom of the press are therefore two entirely correlative things: censorship and universal suffrage are, on the contrary, two things that contradict each other...[66]

De Tocqueville's conclusion that sovereignty of the people and freedom of the press are correlative is simply another way of stating the democracy theory for freedom of speech. If speech is considered to be part of the collective thought process, free speech seems more the natural state of affairs than a revolutionary philosophy. As de Tocqueville observed, you cannot have popular sovereignty without freedom of speech. However, de Tocqueville also noted that while his observation was concerned exclusively with free speech and political matters, he could not help but notice that American newspapers could be without principles and coarsely intrude upon the private lives and reveal "their weaknesses and their vices."[67] This observation today finds its expression in the lack of privacy accorded public persons in the United States as compared to the situation within the European Union.

The Modern Democracy and Self-Government Theory

When he first articulated the democracy or self-government theory in 1948, Alexander Meiklejohn argued that First Amendment free speech applied only to matters directly concerning self-government.[68] An individual, participating in democracy or self-government, must be able to express views and receive views stated by others, all with the goal of making an informed decision.[69] Under this theory, speech relating to criticism and comments about government officials and public policies is accorded the highest degree of protection.[70] There is a logical progression that leads to this conclusion: first, government controlled by the citizens is conducted through elected officials; second, the citizen's primary control over government is through election of public officials; third, speech that informs electoral choice is essential for political control by the citizens, which, in turn, is the goal of democratic government.[71]

However, by 1961, Meiklejohn expanded his free speech theory and moved beyond election-related speech to include many more elements of speech that might indirectly affect as well as directly concern self-government. Consequently, education, science, philosophy, literature, arts, and all manner of individual or group expression could fall within the concept of protected First Amendment free speech if the speech affected self-government.[72] In this expanded mode, it can be somewhat difficult to identify speech that is outside of the sphere of self-government. Professor Meiklejohn's expanded definition of free speech was perhaps not entirely satisfactory because it lacked parameters and was unwieldy. This, of course, raises the issue of how far freedom of speech should extend beyond matters that are purely related to elections and government policies.

More recently, in the context of a privacy case, Baroness Hale of the Supreme Court of the United Kingdom had occasion to list free speech categories and also concluded that "top of the list is political speech." Political speech clearly included information about elected officials that is relevant to their performance as leaders. However, intellectual, educational, and artistic speech are also important because they enable individuals to reach full potential and maximise their participation in the democratic process.[73] In short, Baroness Hale's enumeration starts off staying within the confines of speech directly relating to democratic government, but, like Meiklejohn's expanded list, soon becomes somewhat unwieldy. While Baroness Hale clearly envisaged free speech more like Meiklejohn's expanded explanation, US Judge Robert Bork sought to contain the situation by reverting to Meiklejohn's original concept of free speech that was limited to matters directly related to "governmental behaviour, policy or personnel" and would not include "scientific, educational, commercial or literary expressions" even though they may have an effect on politics.[74] Regardless of how narrowly or broadly the democracy theory is defined, it still focuses on direct or indirect effects on government and invites the conclusion that if considered as an all-inclusive free speech theory, it is ultimately deficient because it simply does not reach enough aspects of life and fails to provide a justification for a broad free speech principle.[75] Viewed as one component of the bundle of free speech rights, the democracy theory is a key element. However, even within this very limited theory, there are nonetheless difficulties in determining the boundaries of free speech.

The difficulty in defining the range of political free speech is demonstrated by examining an example of expressive conduct that falls outside of a direct relationship to self-government but which has abundantly clear political overtones and would require application of Meiklejohn's expanded definition to be protectable free speech. Consider the rather clear political implications of Diego Rivera's famous, incomplete, and short-lived depression era mural, in Rockefeller Center in New York that featured a depiction of Lenin and other socialist themes among workers and capitalists.[76] Rivera was expressing his endorsement or favourable view of Marxist-Leninist philosophy—clearly a political message. Similarly, the destruction of that work of art at the direction of its owners might also be viewed as relating to self-government—their displeasure with communism is certainly political speech.[77] The political message conveyed by the destruction of the mural was the opposition of the Rockefeller family to the Marxist-Leninist ideals endorsed by Rivera. While the conduct of both Rivera and the Rockefellers had clear political implications, it would most surely fall outside of the democracy theory as originally articulated by Meiklejohn and as endorsed by Judge Bork. Nevertheless, the conduct had such clear political overtones that it should be included under Meiklejohn's expanded definition of political speech.

The relationship between free speech and democracy is so close that it has been suggested that it is not possible to understand democracy or free speech without considering them together.[78] Free speech and democracy work together in a number of symbiotic or correlative ways: (1) free speech facilitates citizen involvement in public affairs; (2) free speech promotes discovery of political truth; (3) free speech allows for formation of majorities and majority rule; (4) free exchange of ideas by citizens tempers corruption, and ineptitude, and (5) free speech promotes stability.[79] In other words, free speech empowers the citizens to exercise control and to hold elected officials accountable.[80]

While one of the criticisms of Mill is that truth does not necessarily emerge from freedom of speech, the same criticism cannot be made of the democracy theory because the theory is not diminished if free speech yields something less than a theoretically best result. This is because democracy accords sovereignty to the people, and the sovereign is entitled to be wrong, so the fact that free speech may not contribute to truth is not a compelling criticism.[81] There is, however, a danger that the roar of the crowd or popular exercise of free speech to manage government may impair an unpopular minority's ability to be heard. By injecting another twist to the equation, Ronald Dworkin solves this problem that tends to be inherent in popular rule. Dworkin avoids the consequences of unfettered majoritarian democracy by grafting an element of the individual reason for freedom of speech to the democracy theory and by suggesting that democracy requires that each individual retain a personal right to contribute and participate.[82] By adding this individual right, the risk of a temporary majority restricting any disfavoured group from exercising a right of free speech to espouse possibly extremely unpopular viewpoints is avoided. However, by adding the individual right of dissent, the distinction between the political reason and the individual reason for free speech is blurred, but this is not really a criticism as these theories intersect in any number of places.

The Issue of Democracy and Partnership

A difficulty with the democracy theory as originally espoused is that it does not contemplate the natural inclination of a majority to use its power of free speech to suppress the free speech rights of the minority. So, as a modification of the democracy theory, the concept of democracy and partnership was proposed. The concept of partnership is to limit majoritarian rights so that free speech cannot be used to suppress unpopular speech. In this respect, the availability of free speech may be contrary to the express desires of the majority. While this might seem to have more to do with the structure of democratic government, it also relates directly to freedom of speech. The imperative of recognising speech that could even subvert the interests of the majority and democratic government itself was recognised early in the American Republic. In 1805 in his Second Inaugural Address, Thomas Jefferson acknowledged that the First Amendment even protected speech advocating the destruction of the republic:

> If there be any among us who would wish to dissolve this Union or to change its republican form, let them stand undisturbed as monuments of the safety with which error or opinion may be tolerated where reason is left free to combat it.[83]

By restricting the rights of the majority to suppress unpopular speech, both free speech and democracy are enhanced because majoritarian government is maintained but there is also the freedom to share opinions.[84] The citizens function as equal partners who must be given the same opportunity to shape opinion regardless of what the majority thinks at the time.[85] Using tolerance as the justification, University of Michigan President Lee Bollinger introduced a free speech theory that holds that through the sharing of majority and minority opinions, free speech encourages tolerance which is both a societal and individual virtue.[86] Under this theory, society's acceptance of minority speech augments the society's general character for tolerance.[87] Beyond furnishing free speech with a warm and accommodating dimension, the result is that collective decision-making has the benefit of many opinions and is more fully informed and can, therefore, reach a decision that has considered all viewpoints. The viewpoint of toleration has a clear relationship to Meiklejohn's concept of self-government because both concepts focus on social values—the right to listen and to decide.[88]

Since the US Constitution was written in terms of individual rights, it is unlikely the majoritarian concept of free speech was in the minds of the Framers; the broader partnership concept was probably more likely. The Framers of the American Republic had been committed revolutionaries before enacting the Bill of Rights, and they were accustomed to lively debate to the point that words had stirred them to taking up arms. Since guarantees of freedom of speech disable the majority from reducing or eliminating unpopular speech, guaranteed freedom of speech reduces the political power of the majority and makes political power more equal on a person-by-person basis.[89] Free speech is thus an essential tool in providing equality among citizens.[90] Free speech may therefore be considered an instrument promoting equality and a partnership among citizens. The shift from majoritarian democracy to the concept of equal participation or citizen partnership converts the underlying issue from one of popular sovereignty to a matter of respect for individual dignity.[91] In this respect, the democracy free speech theory overlaps into the individual reason. Free speech not only averts the tyranny of the majority but also permits the individual to express unpopular ideas that ultimately enhance the vibrancy of the democracy.[92] The plurality of opinions fuels Holmes' marketplace of ideas—democracy is a form of government, and government cannot make correct decisions unless it has access to all points of view, even if the majority expressing its rights of free speech would elect to suppress contrary speech. Viewed in this light, all of these arguments are just a limited application of John Stuart Mill's basic tenet of truth emerging from free speech.

British free speech scholar Eric Barendt suggested that when the political reason–based democracy theory is combined with the individual-based reason concepts of dignity and self-fulfilment, the democracy theory "becomes the most influential theory in the development of free speech law."[93] By combining the basic democracy theory with elements of the self-fulfilment and dignity theory, the result is a more comprehensive theory that avoids the risk of suppression of speech by the majority.[94] Ultimately, the formula by which collective speech rights are amalgamated with individual rights will define the structure of the democratic government itself. Free speech is essential for democratic government, and the definition of free speech adopted by each democracy will control how each government operates and relates to its citizens.

Democracy and Distrust of Government

Frederick Schauer has suggested that the natural distrust of government by citizens offers another basis for free speech. This is a rather negative argument based on the so-called natural tendency of governments to suppress speech and dissemble to the populace.[95] Historically, the US government has repeatedly engaged in efforts to suppress free speech that it does not like. This conduct includes the anti-communist Palmer Raids of 1919 and has continued in various forms up to the Patriot Act following the 9/11 terrorist attacks.[96] But whether government fails to embrace freedom of speech through preoccupation with security, nonexistent threats, or possibly through bungling and incompetence more than malice, the result is the same—free speech and the rights of citizens suffer.[97] Sometimes, even the Supreme Court shows its own distrust of governmental agencies by legislating explicit rules in the guise of judicial decisions. Examples include *Mapp v. Ohio,* in which the Supreme Court found that rules governing evidence gathering were being ignored by state officials and therefore an evidentiary exclusionary rule was adopted by the Court to force compliance.[98] Similarly, in *Miranda v. Arizona,* the Supreme Court found that police so invariably violated rights of detained persons that the Court actually crafted or legislated the specific language of mandatory warnings that the police must read to the accused.[99]

The distrust of government in America also explains the reluctance of the American courts to regulate speech content such as hate speech directed against minorities. For example, in 1977, an American Nazi organisation wanted to hold a march in Skokie, Illinois, a Chicago suburb that was home to a large Jewish population, including several thousand Holocaust survivors. The venue was selected to maximise the offensiveness of the expressive conduct, which fell within the umbrella of speech. The City of Skokie reacted by enacting local laws or ordinances to prohibit the rally. In overturning the ordinances and ordering that the march could not be barred, the US Court of Appeals made special mention of the fact that Americans do "not trust any government to separate the true from the false" and restrictions on speech content cannot be permitted.[100] Despite the reluctance of the American courts to regulate hate speech, from a theoretical and empirical standpoint, there remains conflicting evidence as to whether hate speech regulation enhances or diminishes free speech and democratic society.[101]

While hate speech cannot be outlawed in the United States, it can be regulated in special environments such as in the confines of the workplace where it can amount to creating a hostile work environment, in schools or on the university campus[102] and sometimes it may be dealt with in other less heavy-handed ways than outright prohibition. For example, in the late nineteenth century, as police commissioner of the city of New York, Theodore Roosevelt, was confronted with a situation where a virulently anti-Semitic member of the German Reichstag wanted to address the German-speaking citizens of New York. The future President refused entreaties from the Jewish population to prohibit the speech. Rather, Roosevelt created a mockery of the speaker by having him escorted at all times by a phalanx of forty Jewish policemen.[103]

American Realism

American realism or legal realism was an intellectual movement of the 1920s and 1930s that contended that judicial decisions were not so much based on the legal rules cited by the judges but were based, in fact, on the judges' own political and moral predispositions. The rules of law cited in a decision were really rationalisations rather than explanations for the decision.[104] The realists focused on how events really happened as opposed to the formal explanations. Because this school of thought is built on scepticism based on practical experience, it differs conceptually from theory proposed by legal philosophers or theorists. In a sense, it is more of an engineering or mechanical application than it is pure science. American realism is predicated more on how things appear to work in practice rather than on abstract theory and, consequently, is not really a theory at all, but is simply a formal recognition of judicial imprecision that should be appreciated by both theorists and courts.[105] Conceptually it is difficult to place within the philosophical, political, and individual reasons, and it is somewhat elusive within the instrumental and constitutive justifications.

American realism is basically a doctrine that says that restrictions on free speech imposed or enforced by the legal system should be minimised because of the unreliability of the legal system. In a sense, it might attach to any of the reasons for the purpose of expanding or liberalising the application of each reason. It is a negative reason for expanding freedom of expression; namely, rights should be liberally construed because the regulatory mechanisms are so unreliable or defective. It is included in the discussion of political reasons because the argument is inextricably connected to the political system including regulatory agencies, such as the Federal Communications Commission, and the courts, which are also a part of government. Unlike other theories associated with freedom of expression, American realism approaches freedom of speech from the opposite direction—namely, the restrictions, especially defamation—and provides reasons for limiting defamation laws. While difficult to categorise, American realism is nevertheless a significant component of traditional free speech analysis and is included within the political reason because it seems to be most frequently discussed in connection with speech concerning public officials or matters of public interest.

In the context of freedom of expression, American realism is particularly appropriate in terms of yielding an expanded privilege against liability for defamation. Under this approach, a hard and fast rule relegating publication of false facts as being outside of the scope of free speech would inevitably lead to the erosion of free speech because it is naïve to assume that the judicial system always reaches the correct result. As many trial lawyers would agree, it can be difficult to prove the truth of a factual statement even if it is an accurate statement and, even if facts can be proven, the judicial system is far from perfect and errors are made. The point is rather well made by the ability of the late entertainer Liberace to sue a London newspaper successfully for defaming him by daring to raise questions concerning his sexual preferences. Adding insult to injury, the entertainer recovered what was then one of the largest libel verdicts in British history.[106] Perhaps the ultimate bit of realism is that regardless of the rate of error inherent in the judicial system, the costs associated with legal proceedings may simply make it unwise to bother publishing facts that are likely to be challenged. As a matter of pragmatism and commercial reality, without some special protection for speech, a publisher may be punished for publishing a true statement and consequently, to avoid the risk and the expense inherent in legal proceedings, self-censorship may be the inevitable result.[107]

American realism generally supports an expanded freedom of expression privilege on the basis that the legal system is far from perfect and unless society wants to jeopardise essential free speech, common sense considerations dictate that publishers and speakers be given some leeway concerning factual statements before liability attaches. The issues addressed in American realism could be applied on a universal basis because there is no such thing as an infallible or perfectly efficient legal system. Trials are artificial re-creations of events that have already transpired. Trials have evolved with many rules that govern the form that evidence must take if it is to be introduced to judge or jury. One of the most complex areas of trial practice concerns the many rules for the admission and exclusion of hearsay testimony which, by definition, includes all documentary evidence. Hearsay may be defined as an out-of-court statement offered to prove the truth of the matter asserted. Since all documents, including business records, are prepared outside of the court proceedings, they constitute hearsay evidence. In addition to hearsay issues, documents also must pass authentication hurdles. The result is that many items of proof are excluded from consideration by the judge or jury.

In the context of defamation claims, media reporters have frequently relied on confidential sources and, for various reasons, may not be at liberty to disclose those sources. For example, in situations involving reports of organised crime or terrorist activities, the sources might be placed in serious jeopardy if their identities were disclosed. The result is that being able to prove a fact in court and the ultimate truth of the matter may be very different propositions. Since society has decided to resolve disputes between parties through the means of the artificial environment of court trials, it is necessary to recognise the inherent limitations of the trial mechanism.

If a society's underlying philosophy is that free speech has an independent worth that is very high, then recognition of that worth should carry over to the realities of the courtroom. If the underlying value of speech is high and the challenge of developing admissible proof is recognised, then the legal standard should anticipate this situation and give some latitude to authors and publishers. In other words, accept that the mechanism for measuring truth or falsity is imperfect and, give the benefit of the doubt on the side of free speech and permit some level of falsehood so as not to restrain free speech. If someone could devise a method superior to the civil trial for determining truth, then this concept of providing some slack on the side of speech might not be necessary. In addition to imprecision in results, the time and expense of litigation may undoubtedly have some effect on what is published unless some level of falsity is tolerated. If a publisher needed to anticipate the costs of litigation every time a falsehood was published, the natural inclination could be self-censorship to avoid the expense.[108]

In addition to the foibles of legal systems recognised by American realism, there are additional related factors that should be considered that also call for expanded freedom of speech. Mill stated that false ideas had value because they would help to develop better ideas. Mill believed that falsehoods would actually promote discovery of the truth because a false opinion will ultimately yield a "clearer perception and livelier impression of truth" when truth collides with the erroneous belief.[109] While this may or may not be a correct proposition, it is likely correct that inadvertent factual falsehoods or errors may be beneficial or even possess social utility because they give publishers the flexibility they need to promote debate about public issues. Such a social utility approach can be demonstrated both by examining how freedom of speech actually encourages debate and how it facilitates resolution of defamation disputes. As is well recognised under the common law of negligence, the greater the social utility of the activity, the lower the degree of care required.[110] An example is the standard of care for medical practitioners rendering emergency first aid to accident victims. The social utility of encouraging physicians and nurses to render care as volunteers at the scene of accidents is viewed as being of such great social utility as to justify Good Samaritan laws that absolve medical professionals from normal standards of medical practice in connection with the rendering of first aid. Consequently, the *New York Times* case is harmonious with traditional tort law insofar as the Supreme Court has attached a high value to speech regarding public officials.[111] Consequently, the duty of care by the publisher of the defamatory speech is very low.

In the *New York Times* case, the Supreme Court said that erroneous statements need to be protected "if the freedoms of expression are to have the breathing space that they need to survive."[112] In other words, permitting some degree of falsehood without legal recrimination encourages free speech. In engineering terms, since no system can be expected to operate at one hundred percent efficiency, to achieve a certain level or result, the system must have excess capacity. If one of society's goals is to encourage the maximum contribution from an individual, then that individual should not be constrained to say only demonstrably truthful statements. Rather, to elicit all that the individual knows, the individual must be allowed to go beyond what can be proven.

C.The Individual Reason

The individual reason for free speech is based on the dignity of the individual and the right of self-fulfilment.[113] This reason includes numerous theories all of which relate to the individual rather than society at large. All of the theories and reasons deriving from John Stuart Mill relate to free speech helping to progress something such as truth, good government or perhaps even scientific research. The individual reason is a major departure because it posits that free speech is a desirable end unto itself because it is an essential aspect of human autonomy and dignity.[114]

It would be difficult to imagine any concept that more clearly defines the constitutive justification of free speech—free speech is valuable in its own right rather than because of its ability to help achieve some desirable social goal such as democratic government. Many philosophers and scholars have expressed their approval of this concept, and numerous terms have been devised to express the value of free speech to the individual. Some of these terms include self-fulfilment, good character, liberty, and autonomy; and while there may exist subtle distinctions in their meanings, they are, nevertheless, closely related. Even if these ideas are distinct at some level, they can be treated interchangeably because they seem to be aspects of the same continuum of thinking. In a rough sense, all of these terms relate to the emotional or psychological benefits realised by an individual who enjoys rights to freedom of expression.

Philosophers from ancient Greece through Immanuel Kant played key roles in the early development of the constitutive free speech justification. In the modern era, insights have been articulated by well-regarded free speech and legal philosophy scholars such as Lee Bollinger, Alan Haworth, Thomas Scanlon, Vincent Blasi, C.E. Baker, Frederick Schauer, Ronald Dworkin, and many others. Perhaps the most appropriate theory to consider first relates to autonomy. The concept of autonomy is simply the state of not being subject to the will of another and is likely the most complex among the theories considered within those surrounding the individual reason. Connecting the state of autonomy specifically to free speech is not as easily achieved as would be the case with an instrumental theory such as the marketplace of ideas because instrumental theories are based on direct cause and effect relationships. However, individual reasons connect to free speech and, as stated by political philosopher Alan Haworth, language is pervasively woven into "the texture of human life" and consequently cannot be separated from individual autonomy.[115]

Immanuel Kant argued that set dogmas and formulas amounted to balls and chains and that the only escape was the development of free minds. Kant's philosophy maintained that "the public use of man's reason must always be free, and it alone can bring about the enlightenment among men."[116] As will become apparent, this single line from Kant goes to the heart of much of the constitutive free speech justification. Kant envisioned that a legitimate government can only command respect when citizens are equal and autonomous. Free speech plays an important part in being equal and autonomous. By autonomous, Thomas Scanlon explained that a person is autonomous as long as awareness of the state of the law does not settle the question of whether the citizen will comply. That is, the citizen must still be capable of deciding whether or not to comply with the law, recognising the consequences for noncompliance.[117] Kant's vision of autonomy is also related to human dignity as a theory supporting free speech.

Ronald Dworkin has been a leading exponent of the importance of individual human dignity as a basis for free speech. He contends that each person must be treated with equal dignity and respect and as independently valuable. Similarly, the choices of each individual must be accorded equal respect.[118] If each individual is to be accorded equal respect regardless of the merits of their viewpoints, then it follows that the speech, reflecting the thoughts, of each individual must also be respected. When the state suppresses the thoughts, as reflected in the speech, of the individual, injury is done to the individual's dignity.[119] For democracy to function, the free speech rights of the individual must be preserved and not be subject to suppression even if the majority does not want those views expressed. In this respect, the individual reason connects back to the political reason or instrumental justification.

Furthermore, the concept of individual dignity is in harmony with Thomas Scanlon's argument that freedom of speech is essential to protect individual sovereignty and with Kant's belief in autonomy. Scanlon suggested that all decisions, whether required by law or not, must ultimately be made by the individual and therefore the individual must be entitled to collect all relevant information concerning the decision that must be made.[120] Freedom of speech must be assured so as to ensure that the individual makes the best decision concerning the matter at hand. Freedom of speech is essential as a source of choices. This argument focuses on the individual as the listener rather than the speaker.[121] Consequently, the theoretical arguments built around individual sovereignty are not so much an explanation of the right to speak but of the right to listen, and at its root the theory is predicated on inherent dignity or rights of the individual.[122] Kant's autonomy argument has also been recast in terms of free speech nurturing good character among citizens. Freedom of expression may nurture inquisitiveness, initiative, and courage.'[123] Conversely, it could also be argued that freedom of expression enables individuals so disposed to join in evil activities and go along with the crowd. From a legal perspective, it would seem that freedom of expression, for better or worse, enables the individual to pursue the individual's goals whether they are beneficial or harmful.

The liberty theory, not to be confused with the democracy theory, which is a political reason as opposed to being an individual reason, also has clear connections to the concept of autonomy. C. Edwin Baker developed the liberty theory as an alternative to the instrumental marketplace of ideas. In this approach, free speech is protected because of its value to the individual and is part of the essential liberty of each individual. Like the other constitutive justifications, liberty is not so much a means to an end but is an end unto itself.[124] The liberty theory holds the value of free speech to be intensely personal.[125]

Under the liberty theory, all of the First Amendment rights—speech, press, assembly, and religion—are actually just "different markers" on the same theme of freedom of self-expression and self-determination.[126] In certain respects, the liberty theory crosses over from constitutive to instrumental justification. Free speech promotes the speaker's self-fulfilment and enables the speaker to influence the course of events.[127] This theory presents exciting theoretical implications because what starts as a constitutive justification undergoes a metamorphosis into an instrumental justification as the speaker's individual liberty influences others in a democratic decision-making process. However, the liberty theory may be criticised to the extent that it is not so much a new theory but is a new term defined so broadly as to subsume other theories. To the extent that it is defined to embrace both instrumental and constitutive justifications, it would not be surprising that it can explain more situations than any individual theory or justification. Indeed, the liberty theory in its various iterations approximates the results from a sociological perspective.

The connection between personal liberty and free speech was perhaps most eloquently addressed in Justice Louis Brandeis' concurring opinion in *Whitney v. California*, in which he made a stirring plea for free speech in terms of personal liberty:

> Those who won our independence believed that the final end of the state was to make men free to develop their faculties; and that in its government the deliberative forces should prevail over the arbitrary. *They valued liberty both as an end and as a means.* They believed liberty to be the secret of happiness and courage to be the secret of liberty. They believed that freedom to think as you will and to speak as you think are means indispensable to the discovery and spread of political truth; that without free speech and assembly discussion would be futile; that with them, discussion affords ordinarily adequate protection against the dissemination of noxious doctrine; that the greatest menace to freedom is an inert people; that public discussion is a political duty; and that this should be a fundamental principle of the American government.[128]

Brandeis' words, while speaking in terms of liberty, hearken back to truth and democracy as well, demonstrating how all of the three reasons are ultimately inter-related. The liberty theory specifically references the value of speech as a form of self-fulfilment, an individual reason, while Brandeis connects liberty to both political and philosophical reasons.

Self-fulfilment theory by its own terms focuses on the individual and not the state or society.[129] This approach holds that each individual has the right to free speech as a matter of self-gratification even though the exercise of that right may not be in the interest of society.[130] However, there are arguments that the theory is insufficient because free speech simply cannot be equated with pleasure or happiness in a general way given that the public accepts substantial and intrusive government regulation of many activities which involve happiness and self-fulfilment yet does not accept such pervasive regulation of speech. Freedom of speech therefore requires some additional justification for not tolerating intervention.[131] Individuals enjoy and require food, shelter, security, health care, and any number of other physical goods. Yet, the government is allowed to intrude in all of these areas. Governments regulate speed limits on motorways, prescribe the minimum age for purchasing alchohol, license medical practitioners, prescribe medical school curricula, certify drugs, license dogs and cats; yet none of this conduct is perceived as a violation of basic human rights. If speech were regulated to the same extent as owning a dog or health care, it would be disingenuous to talk about a free speech principle.

There is another fundamental limitation of the self-fulfilment theory—it does not account for freedom of the press or other business entities that presumably do not have an intrinsic need for self-fulfilment.[132] This argument appears compelling because freedom of speech frequently involves large media organisations. It is invariably the case with respect to defamation in which the culpable parties include not only an author but also a corporate publisher or broadcaster. Just as the democracy theory tends to be somewhat circumscribed by political discussion, self-fulfilment is also limited because it does not include all varieties of speakers. However, in response to this criticism, it is necessary to consider that the media, like all corporate entities, operates through individuals, including strong-willed editors or even media barons or moguls who have interests in media content. In defence of the self-fulfilment theory, it must also be recognised that the apparent failings are not so much failings as limitations. The self-fulfilment theory may not include all aspects of free speech but is useful to the extent that it explains free speech with respect to the individual. However, the criticism that the theory is inadequate because individuals willingly accept government regulation of many other forms of self-gratification, such as operating motor vehicles at excessive speed and consumption of alcohol, is far more troubling. A theory based on self-gratification, like other individual theories, appears to be inadequate to explain the special status accorded free speech.

Feminist jurisprudence has raised some timely and special concerns with traditional perspectives of free speech and focuses special concern on pornography and hate speech.[133] A tenet of feminist analysis is that speech is free for some but not free for others. Speech advocating or praising sexual violence or debasement of women is by no means free expression for the targets who are all too frequently victims of this type of speech. In this regard, traditional approaches to free speech fail to recognise that white male heterosexuals are not the only members of humanity and that speech that quells the voice of everyone else is hardly free.[134] Feminism challenges two pillars of free speech theory: truth and autonomy. Feminist theory projects that truth and autonomy are "incoherent, impossible and dangerous."[135] Arguably, the flaw with traditional theory is that it is gender biased because conventional freedom of speech has been routinely used in the humiliation of women and minorities.[136]

The feminist approach has attracted a number of advocates and has enriched the free speech dialogue by involving realities of human existence in a social context. One of the concerns raised by the feminist approach is that pornography not only demeans women but also constitutes an "act" rather than pure speech in that it is a physical mechanism for the abuse, mortification, and debasement of women to satisfy male desires.[137] In addition to feminist analysis, the same arguments concerning other disempowered minorities can also be supported. Because free speech may tend to further the oppression of minorities, arguments have been presented that would authorise government to engage in a more thorough analysis before authorising such abusive speech.[138] While the feminist arguments raise substantial issues, from an American legal standpoint, it must be recognised that the First Amendment simply will not wear many of the feminist arguments because they are simply far too content based and therefore the arguments are difficult to apply in the context of law as opposed to a human rights discussion.

Conclusion - A Synthesis of Free Speech Theories

Having considered numerous arguments in support of free speech, this chapter suggests that among the classical theories, Mill's concept of truth and Kant's theory of autonomy are really the essential theories that support the instrumental and constitutive justifications for freedom of speech. While truth may not be the ineluctable consequence of free speech, free speech is nevertheless desirable because it is the best overall method for individuals and societies to make good choices. If "good choices" were substituted for "truth," it is likely that Mill's arguments would be more compelling and less subject to criticism. While good choices are not necessarily the same as discovering the truth, good choices are, by definition, at least a step in the right direction. Appreciating that truth is not necessarily something fixed for all time, free speech provides unrestricted access to information from which both listener and speaker can benefit and make informed decisions. It is important to note that the chosen phrase is that the parties *can* benefit, not that they necessarily will benefit. This is invariably the result because free speech includes the autonomy or liberty to make incorrect choices while being aware of the consequences. But, and this is the overriding concern, free speech optimises choice by maximising the known options. Similarly, free speech gives the individual autonomy, including basic liberty to hold opinions, to make choices, and to participate in public debate when so inclined.

Perhaps "truth" is simply not the best word—it is too absolute for our relativistic times and "good choices" has a condescending implication. Mill was living in a world defined by Newtonian absolutes and universal laws. Just as Victorian writers like Kipling displayed no doubts as to the correctness of imperialist colonialism as a means of bringing civilisation to what they perceived as more primitive cultures, Mill could be assured that truth would emerge from free speech. Today, it is no longer possible to look at situations with such assurance—not because free speech is not working in the right direction, but rather because people of the twenty-first century are uncomfortable with absolutes indicated by words like "truth." A possible restatement of Mill's general proposition might be that free speech is desirable because it promotes critical thinking. The concept of critical thinking as opposed to truth might seem to be a radical departure but the two concepts have a connection. If we accept that ultimate truths are difficult or impossible to isolate and may not even exist, but critical thinking, even with missteps, moves the world away from ignorance; then free speech may find its justification in that it promotes rational thinking in both listener and speaker. If thinking is desirable, so too must be free speech. Whether directed towards affairs of government or in the reviews of a new restaurant, freedom of speech enhances the ability to make informed, though not necessarily optimal, choices. This enhancement may be the ultimate worth of free speech.

It has been suggested that the concept of individual self-realisation encompasses all of the free speech arguments. Self-realisation is viewed as encompassing both the individual's achievement of full-potential and the individual's control of personal destiny. Of course, the phrase, self-realisation, has the benefit of being somewhat ambiguous or amorphous.[139] From a theoretical point of view, this is not just a matter of semantics because the self-realisation argument has as its goal dispelling the notion that freedom of expression encompasses a complex set of values.[140] But self-realisation is not a complete explanation because free speech as a component of democracy is more of a societal benefit than it is individual. It has also been suggested that free speech might be explained as being required by democratic culture which, in turn, is defined as encompassing personal liberty as well as democratic government.[141] The idea that freedom of expression is ultimately a cultural phenomenon begins the process of moving freedom of expression away from the exclusive realm of the legal theorist and sets the stage for harmonising the philosophical and legal concepts with sociological theory, the subject of the following chapter.

ENDNOTES

1. Keith Werhan, *Freedom of Speech—A Reference Guide to the United States Constitution*, 28–40.
2. Ronald Dworkin, *Freedom's Law: The Moral Reading of the American* Constitution, 199–200.
3. Ibid., 200.
4. D.F.B. Tucker, *Law, Liberalism and Free Speech*, 9–30.
5. Frederick Schauer, "The Role of the People in First Amendment Theory", *California Law Review* 74 (1986): 761, 769. In this article, Schauer discusses consequential and deontological perspectives on free speech in the special context of the role of juries.
6. Daniel Farber, *The First Amendment*, 6.
7. Thomas I. Emerson, *The System of Freedom of Expression.*
8. Thomas Tedford and Dale Herbeck, *Freedom of Speech in the United States*, 437–439.
9. Ibid., 432.
10. Ibid.
11. Frederick Schauer, *Free Speech: A Philosophical* Enquiry, 15.
12. John Stuart Mill, *On Liberty*, 12.
13. C. Edwin Baker, "Scope of the First Amendment Freedom of Speech", *University of California Law Review* 25 (1977–1978): 964.
14. Ibid.
15. *Abrams v. US,* 250 US 616, 630-631 (1919) (dissenting opinion).
16. In 409 BCE, Euripedes wrote that true liberty exists "when free born men, having to advise the public, may speak free…." Louis Ingelhart (ed), *Press and Speech Freedoms in the World from Antiquity Until 1998—A Chronology* (Westport, London: Greenwood Press, 1998) 4.
17. Garrett Epps (ed), *The First Amendment Freedom of the Press*, 29.
18. George Anastaplo, *Reflections on Freedom of Speech and the First Amendment*, 21.
19. John Milton, *Areopagitica,* 54.
20. Robert Hargreaves, *A History of Free Speech*, 100–101.
21. Robert Trager and Donna Dickerson, *Freedom of Expression in the 21st Century,* 47–49.
22. Harry M. Bracken, *Freedom of Speech–Words Are Not Deeds*, 10.
23. Michael Curtis, *Free Speech, 'The People's Darling Privilege'*, 35.

24. Ibid., 37.
25. John Trenchard and Thomas Gordon, *Cato's letters: essays on liberty, civil and religious, and other important matters* (1720), quoted in Hargreaves, *A History of Free Speech*, 151.
26. Curtis, 45–46.
27. Thomas Paine, *The Age of Reason*, dedication page.
28. Ibid., 195.
29. Mill, 13.
30. Ibid., 20.
31. Ibid., 55.
32. Raphael Cohen-Almagor, *Speech, Media, and Ethics: The limits of Free Expression*, 5.
33. Douglas Fraleigh and Joseph Tuman, *Freedom of Speech in the Market-place of* Ideas, 13–15; Wojciech Sadurski, *Freedom of Speech and Its Limits*, 8.
34. H.L. Pohlman, *Justice Oliver Wendell Holmes—Free Speech and the Living* Constitution, 10.
35. *Abrams,* 250 US 616, 630-631 (1919).
36. Anthony Lewis, *Make No Law—The Sullivan Case and the First Amendment*, 81.
37. *Abrams,* 250 US 616, 630 (1919).
38. *Gitlow v. New York,* 268 US 652 (1925).
39. 376 US 254 (1964) ("*New York Times*").
40. *Brandenburg v. Ohio*, 395 US 444, 447 (1969).
41. Eric Barendt, *Freedom of Speech,* 9.
42. Schauer, *Free Speech*, 19.
43. Ibid., 21–30.
44. Hargreaves, 303.
45. Baker, 974–981.
46. Zechariah Chafee, Jr., *Free Speech in the United States*, 559–561.
47. Schauer, *Free Speech*, 16.
48. Ibid.
49. Ibid., 27.
50. Frederick Schauer, "The Political Incidence of the Free Speech Principle", *Univ. of Colorado Law Review* 64 (1993): 935.
51. Baker, 981–990.
52. Steven Shiffrin, "The Politics of the Mass Media and the Free Speech Principle", *Indiana Law Journal* 69 (1994): 689, 719.
53. Owen Fiss, *The Irony of Free Speech*, 3.

54. Cass Sunstein, "Free Speech Now", *University of Chicago Law Review* 59 (1992): 255, 301.
55. Madison was clearly of the view that freedom of speech had special significance in political discussions in a democracy. Cass Sunstein, *Democracy and the Problem of Free Speech,* xvi–xvii.
56. The First Amendment embodied what have been termed natural rights that were not granted by the sovereign but were an inalienable part of humanity itself. Steven Heyman, *Free Speech & Human Dignity,* 11–15.
57. David Rabban, *Free Speech in Its Forgotten Years*, 13.
58. *United States Declaration of Independence*, (1776) para 2, as unanimously adopted by the Thirteen Colonies 4 July 1776. While ostensibly drafted by a committee, the first draft was almost in its entirety the work of Thomas Jefferson.
59. See Robert Verkaik, "Royal Family Granted New Right of Secrecy," *The Independent*, (London), 8 January 2011.
60. Lewis, 55.
61. While the Sedition Act expired on its own terms only a few years later, various forms of muzzling criticism of government were implemented from time to time, usually during time of war. See, David Anderson, "Freedom of the Press in Wartime", *University of Colorado Law Review* 77 (2006): 49. Richard Nixon and his infamous lists of "enemies" stand in ignominious contrast to Washington's tolerance of critics.
62. Anthony Lewis, *Freedom for the Thought that We Hate: A Biography of the First Amendment*, 11–21.
63. Hargreaves, 181.
64. George Hay, *Hortensius, An Essay on the Liberty of the Press* (1799, reprinted in www.fjc.gov/history/sedition.nsf/page/hay_pamphlet).
65. Hargreaves, 182. The English common law did not reach the conclusion that government could not be libelled until 1993 when the House of Lords so ruled in *Derbyshire County Council v. Times Newspapers Ltd* [1993] AC 534 [HL].
66. Alexis de Tocqueville, *Democracy in America*, 173–174.
67. Ibid., 177. Overall, de Tocqueville was quite amazed with American newspapers that operated without any type of licensure or control and which proliferated wherever there was advertising to be sold: at 175–177.
68. Alexander Meiklejohn, *Free Speech and its Relation to Self-Government.* There are a number of scholars who still adhere to this limited application of First Amendment free speech theory. See discussion in Cynthia Estlund, "Speech on Matters of Public Concern: The Perils of an Emerging

First Amendment Theory" (1990) 59 *George Washington Law Review* 1, fn12.

69. Richard Moon, *The Constitutional Protection of Freedom of Expression*, 27.
70. Schauer, *Free Speech*, 37.
71. Paul Mitchell, "Malice in Qualified Privilege", *Public Law* (1999): 328, 336.
72. Alexander Meiklejohn, "The First Amendment is an Absolute", *Supreme Court Review* (1961): 245, 256–257.
73. *Campbell v. MGN Ltd* [2004] 2 AC 457, 499-500 [HL].
74. Robert Bork, "Neutral Principles and Some First Amendment Problems", *Indiana Law Journal* 47 (1971): 1, 26–28.
75. Schauer, *Free Speech*, 44.
76. See Cary Reich, *The Life of Nelson A. Rockefeller—Worlds to Conquer 1908–1958*, 106–111.
77. The actual theme of the mural was "Man at the Crossroads Looking with Hope and High Vision to the Choosing of a New and Better Future." The dramatic destruction of the mural on the instruction of the Rockefeller family is recreated in the motion picture *Frida* (2002). A somewhat eccentric attempt to re-create Rivera's mural can be seen on the wall in Gould's bookstore near the University of Sydney campus on King Street in Newtown, NSW Australia. The re-created mural, complete with image of Lenin, is also a political statement not only by its content but also by the very act of its re-creation as signifying defiance by the proprietor of the bookstore.
78. Ronald Dworkin, *Sovereign Virtue: The Theory and Practice of Equality*, 354.
79. Rodney Smolla, *Free Speech in an Open Society*, 12–13.
80. Schauer, *Free Speech*, 38.
81. Ibid., 40.
82. Dworkin, *Sovereign Virtue*, 357–365.
83. By contrast, nearly two hundred years later, Richard Nixon, in a speech in the US House of Representatives said: "we must bear in mind that the rights of free speech and free press do not carry with them the right to advocate the destruction of the very Government which protects the freedom of the individual to express his views." Fawn Brodie, *Richard Nixon—The Shaping of His Character*, 188.
84. Dworkin, 78, 357.

85. Ibid., 364. Schauer reached the same conclusion through equality or equal participation. See Schauer, *Free Speech*, 40–41.
86. Lee Bollinger, *The Tolerant Society: Freedom of Speech and Extremist Speech in America*, 104–144. See Lee Bollinger and Geoffrey Stone (eds.), *Eternally Vigilant—Free Speech in the Modern Era*, 11.
87. Sadurski, 31–32.
88. The relationships of Meiklejohn's and Holmes' free speech theories to Bollinger's concept of tolerance are discussed in Lee Bollinger, "Free Speech and Intellectual Values", *Yale Law Journal* 92 (1983): 438, 454–468.
89. Ronald Dworkin, *A Matter of Principle*, 62–63.
90. Ibid.
91. Schauer, *Free Speech*, 41.
92. Hargreaves, 304–305.
93. Barendt, 20.
94. Ibid.
95. Ibid., 21.
96. See Christopher Finan, *From the Palmer Raids to the Patriot Act: A History of the Fight for Free Speech in America*, 1–37, 268–305.
97. Schauer, *Free Speech*, 86.
98. *Mapp v. Ohio,* 367 US 643 (1961).
99. *Miranda v. Arizona*, 384 US 436 (1966).
100. *Collin v. Smith,* 578 F 2d 1197 (7th Cir 1978).
101. See James Weinstein, *Hate Speech, Pornography and the Radical Attack on Free Speech Doctrine.*
102. Jon Gould, *Speak No Evil: The Triumph of Hate Speech Regulation*, 76–79. The issues concerning extreme speech in general are comprehensively discussed in Ivan Hare & James Weinstein (eds), *Extreme Speech and Democracy.* See also Kenneth Lasson, "To Stimulate, Provoke, or Incite? Hate Speech and the First Amendment" in Monroe Freedman & Eric Freedman (eds), *Group Defamation and Freedom of Speech: The Relationship Between Language and Violence*, 267.
103. John Peters, *Courting the Abyss: Free Speech and the Liberal Tradition*, 158–159. *The New York Times* even joined in the ridicule by printing stories that the anti-Semite's daughter was involved in a romantic relationship with a Jewish young man.
104. Ronald Dworkin, *Taking Rights Seriously*, 3.
105. See Schauer, *Free Speech*, 170. Schauer stated that the contributions of Judge Jerome Frank are particularly apt in defamation disputes. Judge

Frank served on the US Court of Appeals during the mid-twentieth century and was one of the pioneers of the legal realism school of thought. His contributions were undoubtedly influenced by his practical experience of serving over fifteen years as an appellate judge and reviewing trial court decisions.

106. *Liberace v. Daily Mirror Newspapers*, reported in *The Times*, 18 June 1959.
107. Schauer, *Free Speech*, 170.
108. Dario Milo has proposed a number of alternatives to civil litigation that would permit claimants to clear their names without subjecting publishers to "defamation law's obsession with damages." Dario Milo, *Defamation and Freedom of Speech*, 264.
109. Mill, 20.
110. *Restatement of Torts (Second)* (1965) s 291.
111. Nadine Strossen, "A Defence of the Aspirations–But Not the Achievements–of the US Rules Limiting Defamation Actions by Public Officials or Public Figures", *Melbourne University Law Review* 15 (1985–1986): 419, 424–425.
112. 376 US 254, 271-272 (1964) citing *Cantwell v. Connecticut,* 310 US 296, 310 (1940).
113. Tedford and Harbeck, 434.
114. Smolla, 9.
115. Alan Haworth, *Free Speech*, 220. Haworth stated that in the modern era, Thomas Scanlon has made a significant attempt to connect autonomy with freedom of expression: at 218–219.
116. Ibid., 218, citing from Immanuel Kant, *An Answer to the Question: What Is Enlightenment?* in Hans Reis (ed), *Kant's Political Writings*.
117. Thomas Scanlon, "A Theory of Freedom of Expression", *Philosophy & Public Affairs* 1 (1972): 204, 214–215.
118. Dworkin, 200–201.
119. Schauer, *Free Speech*, 62.
120. Thomas Scanlon, "Freedom of Expression and Categories of Expression", *University of Pittsburgh Law Review* 40 (1979): 519. See Harry Wellington, "On Freedom of Expression", *Yale Law Journal* 88 (1978–1979): 1105, 1123–1125.
121. The central role of the listener in free speech theory is discussed comprehensively in Michael Gillooly, *The Third Man—Reform of the Australasian Defamation Defences*.
122. Schauer, *Free Speech*, 71.

123. Vincent Blasi, "Free Speech and Good Character: From Milton to Brandeis to the Present" in Bollinger and Stone (eds.), *Eternally Vigilant—Free Speech in the Modern Era*, 61, 62–63.
124. C. Edwin Baker, *Human Liberty and Freedom of Speech*, 5.
125. Baker, "Scope of the First Amendment Freedom of Speech", 966.
126. Ibid.
127. Baker, *Human Liberty*, 69.
128. *Whitney v. California,* 274 US 357, 375 (1927) (emphasis added).
129. Schauer *Free Speech*, 48.
130. Barendt, 13.
131. Ibid.
132. Ibid., 15.
133. See Judith Butler, *Excitable Speech: A Politics of the Performative* (a linguistic as opposed to strictly legal viewpoint).
134. Robert Jensen & Elvia Arriola, "Feminism and Free Expression: Silence and Voice" in David Allen & Robert Jensen (eds), *Freeing the First Amendment: Critical Perspectives on Freedom of Expression*, 197–199.
135. Susan Williams, *Truth, Autonomy, and Speech: Feminist Theory and the First Amendment*, 3.
136. Ibid.
137. For a questioning examination of this issue, see Franklyn Haiman, *Speech Acts and the First Amendment*, 49–61.
138. See Chris Demaske, *Modern Power and Free speech: Contemporary Culture and Issues of Equality*, 197–202.
139. Martin Redish, "The Value of Free Speech", *University of Pennsylvania Law Review* 130 (1981–1982): 591, 593–596.
140. Ibid., 594.
141. Jack Balkin, "Digital Speech and Democratic Culture: A Theory of Freedom of Expression for the Information Society" *New York University Law Review* 79 (2004): 1, 3–4.

CHAPTER 6

SOCIOLOGY AND LEGAL PHILOSOPHY

HARMONY OR DISCORD?

Having separately examined both traditional arguments for freedom of expression and sociological arguments, the obvious next step is some type of harmonisation or comparison.[1] Essentially, the sociological argument for freedom of expression can be applied in two discussions:

- Freedom of expression can be explained and interpreted through the use of sociological theory without recourse to legal philosophy.
- Sociological theory can be used in the framework of traditional free speech theory to support theories based on the instrumental justification and to show that the theories falling within the constitutive justification are also instrumental theories when applied to society as opposed to the individual.

These points will be separately considered with every effort being made to avoid distorting legal and sociological theories to conform to comparisons. This presents some challenges because the theoretical frameworks are different and, at times, it may seem that round pegs are being squeezed into square holes. This is a potential problem in every comparative study but intellectual squeezing is sometimes permissible, providing that logical contortion does not morph into outright distortion.

FREEDOM OF EXPRESSION EXPLAINED USING SOCIOLOGICAL THEORY

Freedom of expression can be explained and interpreted through the use of sociological theory without recourse to legal philosophy

The first argument really goes to the thesis of this book—that the need for legal rights assuring freedom of expression can be explained through sociological theory as an alternative to more traditional legal philosophy. The central argument is that social theory developed by Emile Durkheim and Jurgen Habermas provides a comprehensive argument for freedom of expression and constitutes a sufficient logical basis for crafting laws and statements of human rights. The concept is fundamentally distinct from other freedom of expression discussions because it is predicated on social theory not usually associated with freedom of speech, and the argument is focused on the needs of society rather than individuals. In this discussion, the concept of society as an institution is based on Durkheim's belief that society is something distinctly different than a sum of its constituent citizens and is an entity or phenomenon that displays its own characteristics.

Central to the sociological discussion is that members of modern democratic, industrial societies require substantial rights to freedom of expression or the society itself will be unable to function and meet the needs of its population. The argument follows a progression of ideas from Durkheim to Habermas, which can be summarised in the following sequence:

- In societies where mechanical solidarity predominates, there is little division of labour and beliefs and values are uniform among citizens. (Durkheim)
- As division of labour increases, society moves from where mechanical solidarity predominates to a situation of organic solidarity. (Durkheim)

- In societies where organic solidarity predominates, shared cultural beliefs and values diminish and individuation increases in direct proportion to the increase in division of labour, reflecting different perceptions and interests of each citizen. (Durkheim)
- Organic solidarity is based not on unity of thought and functions among citizens but on the supportive inter-relationships among members of the society in which division of labour prevails and the citizens perform different functions in which they rely on and support each other. (Durkheim)
- As individuation increases in step with division of labour, society requires the reaching of consensus among the different viewpoints of its members in order for society to function and maintain stability and accomplish common goals such as lawmaking and democratic government. (Habermas)
- Consensus requires that members of society or affinity groups within society engage in communicative action and discuss and thereby have the opportunity to express opinions, listen to various opinions, and have their viewpoints both listened to and treated with respect by other citizens. (Habermas)

Modern democracies require freedom of expression both politically and economically because of the profound and ever-increasing division of labour which creates more and more separate perspectives on virtually every issue. When everyone was a hunter-gatherer, everyone had the same concerns. But, in a world where some people such as American farmers want to promote free trade while others such as steelworkers support protectionism, different viewpoints proliferate. Yet, in this environment which, in Durkheim's language, is held together organically as opposed to mechanically, the multitude of voices must be able to work cooperatively or the underlying division of labour itself is in jeopardy because division of labour only works where the social gears mesh smoothly. In Habermas's worldview, lifeworld (consisting of the members of society) and system (consisting of forces embedded in society that are imposed by power structures) are unified in more simple cultures whereas they diverge in more complex societies.[2] This necessarily follows because in more basic societies where mechanical solidarity prevails, all goals are common goals shared by all the members of the society. As society grows more complex and is predominated by organic solidarity and shared values decline, power structures become more coercive as they must channel increasingly diverse interests within the lifeworld.

Durkheim's arguments for freedom of expression are derived from the nature of organic solidarity found in modern industrial or postindustrial societies. As division of labour increases, each individual obtains greater personal rights—individuality and personality correspondingly increase with the division of labour itself. Growth in division in labour requires that individuals be permitted to develop individuality without hindrance. In other words, speech must be free. If the law fails to accommodate this freedom, it will be out of synch with societal requirements and a state of disharmony or imbalance will eventually result.

Using this theoretical argument, it should be reasonably clear that freedom of expression must be supported or unacceptable stresses will accumulate in the society (Durkheim) or lifeworld (Habermas). Public policy will not be effective unless it takes into consideration the different concerns of individuals or groups sharing the same concerns. The division of labour that permits individuals to specialise in wheat growing or steelmaking also requires a social framework that supports both activities. From the viewpoint of free markets, communication is essential so that supply and demand approximate each other. Public policy needs to reflect the legitimate but different concerns of people occupying different social and economic positions. While freedom of expression belongs to individuals, its ultimate value is to society—freedom of speech is a mechanism for achieving social solidarity in systems typified by individuation, which in turn, is an inevitable result of different perspectives caused by division of labour itself.

Freedom of expression is not an unlimited right because it exists to allow social consensus and when expression is contrary to reaching consensus, the speech rights may be harmful. Consequently, sociological theory admits to restraints on speech that injure people such as hate speech or which offend the conscience collective such as child pornography. The needs for freedom of speech will be determined by the extent of the social division of labour in each society. For example, in a society where everyone belongs to the same religious denomination, freedom of religion is relatively unimportant because there is no social division of labour and mechanical solidarity prevails with respect to religion. As the division of labour increases with respect to any aspect of human existence, the need for freedom of expression within that aspect of existence must also increase in order to provide a mechanism for reaching consensus among disparate views. It should come as no surprise that freedom of expression reaches its zenith in the United States of America where there is an enormous and highly specialised population.

Sociological Theory and Traditional Free Speech

Sociological theory can be used in the framework of traditional free speech discussions to support theories based on the instrumental justification and to show that the theories falling within the constitutive justification are also instrumental theories when applied to society as opposed to the individual.

While probably being better suited as a stand-alone or independent basis for freedom of expression, the Durkheim/Habermas argument discussed previously can also be utilised in connection with more traditional approaches to freedom of expression. In this application, sociological inquiry seeks to support instrumentally based free speech theories and to demonstrate that all or at least most of the theories found within the constitutive justification are in fact properly instrumental when applied to society at large as opposed to just the individual. In this context, sociological theory is demonstrably quite useful in that it transforms the inherently individualistic constitutive theories into theories exhibiting substantial public, as opposed to only personal, benefit. From a practical viewpoint, this transformation can be significant. To date, doctrinal law is much more inclined to recognise instrumentally based free speech theories than the theories falling within the constitutive justification. While this may be the result of the relative specificity of results-oriented instrumental arguments as opposed to the more sweeping moral residue falling within the constitutive justification, it may also reflect belief among lawmakers that the constitutive theories are simply too esoteric for enactment into law.

Traditional instrumental theories almost always relate to political speech and involve group behaviour. The sociological arguments discussed in chapter 2 include political conversation but are more far-ranging and are philosophically much more at home with the theories found within the constitutive justification. However, the constitutive justification is inherently personal—freedom of speech is required for the self-fulfilment of the individual or development of individual autonomy. After making some comparisons, it will be apparent that the sociological approach is actually an argument that, in the context of complex societies exhibiting extensive division of labour, the theories within the constitutive justification can be reclassified within the instrumental justification because they help to accomplish societal goals by initially benefitting individuals. Using Durkheim's metaphor of the human body, freedom of expression energises each individual just as vitamins power each cell with the result that the society or body exhibits greater health and vigour.

Durkheim saw freedom of expression as an essential aspect of individualisation and Habermas regarded it as an essential component of consensus. The two concepts are related because individuation, a necessary component of the social division of labour, in turn, requires a mechanism for achieving consensus in order for organic solidarity to function as society and not just as an anarchic collection of unrelated individuals. Durkheim's concept of organic solidarity—extreme social division of labour with a diminishing amount of commonly held values—requires the type of consensus behaviour envisaged by Habermas. Although Durkheim's analysis does not seem to flow easily into one or more of the existing free speech theories, it does lead into the more developed theoretical models proposed by Habermas.

While Durkheim's rather simplistic approach has the obvious advantage of clarity, the potential utilisation of sociological reasoning is more attainable through some of the concepts of Habermas because he includes communicative action and discourse as central theoretical elements. Although Habermas created complex (and sometimes virtually opaque) sociological models, the underlying concepts are virtually identical to Durkheim's understanding of mechanical and organic solidarity. Habermas viewed traditional societies as being held together by shared values whereas "modern societies are complex, differentiatiated and multicultural" and are not held together by any single "tradition, world view, or set of rules."[3] Habermas then argued that communication is the primary mechanism for social integration in a modern society.[4] Habermas conceptualised the individual living within the lifeworld which is governed by consensus reached through communicative action and discourse; but beyond this lifeworld exists the system which applies an external force on inhabitants of the lifeworld. Theoretical concepts such as lifeworld and system are far removed from Durkheim's more basic theoretical universe and are, in fact, exterior to Habermas's arguments for why freedom of expression is required in today's modern and differentiated lifeworld. However, the concept of system is integral to Habermas's theoretical view because it is through the system that lifeworld conduct is channelled.

Judiciously, Habermas straddled the sociological worlds of both Weber and Durkheim in that he saw society as a collection of individuals (Weber) and as a unique and distinct organism (Durkheim). This almost magically unites the theories lying within the constitutive justification as being both collectively and individually focused. Habermas's recognition that shared values predominate in primitive society is clearly at ease with Durkheim's perspective that individuality does not exist in a primitive state of mechanical solidarity but increases as a function of the division of labour in complex societies held together through organic solidarity. It follows that in a society of hunter-gatherers where mechanical solidarity predominates, the theories within the constitutive justification which deal with individual autonomy will have little or no social value because (1) individual autonomy by and large does not exist where mechanical solidarity predominates and (2) there is no need for common consensus because everyone already shares the same beliefs and values.

Habermas regarded speech as a device to mediate conflict among autonomous individuals in a complex society. To him, freedom of expression is critical because it promotes both discussion and acceptance. As individualism increases, communication becomes essential for agreement. In the more primitive state where mechanical solidarity predominates, communication leading toward consensus is unnecessary because everyone is already in agreement. In summary, in complex societies where organic solidarity predominates, the individual, who resides in the lifeworld, becomes increasingly autonomous—some would say alienated from other members of the lifeworld—and the overall society cannot operate unless individuals can mediate their beliefs through discourse.

The individual right to freedom of expression is the means to mediate or transform a collection of individuals into functional society. Habermas composed formal rules for discourse. The rules distil into a few concepts, namely, everyone is allowed to express personal views, everyone is allowed to question the views of others, and there is no outside coercion applied to speakers, listeners or questioners. Through this process of discourse, Habermas believed that consensus leading to happy and fulfilling lives emerges. This is not too far afield from John Stuart Mill's belief that truth would emerge from free debate. Habermas was not so concerned with finding ultimate truth but is content that discourse can lead to happy life.

Free speech theories found within both instrumental and constitutive justifications are needed to support effective social systems. The instrumental/constitutive dichotomy which seems to work reasonably well among free speech theorists is perhaps not so useful in a sociological examination because from a sociological point of view, theory is useful to the extent that it explains actual behaviour and in that sense, all of the applicable theories become instrumental or results-oriented at the societal level. Starting with the application of sociology to free speech falling within the instrumental justification, it is evident that discourse theory supports freedom of political speech. Given that the goal of discourse is consensus, the application in election contests is very clear. Individuals and candidates debate public issues and from these free and open discussions, the greater public is able to reach decisions. But Habermas makes no such limitation as political argument. Discourse can and should be about movies, books, art, music, and virtually anything else that interests a group of people. Both Habermas and Durkheim envisaged that a great deal of this discourse would occur within the confines of affinity groups, both formal and informal, everything from trade unions to ad hoc groups gathered in a coffee house or pub.

Following the order of theoretical discussion in the preceding chapter, an appropriate place to begin is John Stuart Mill's truth theory. Mill argued that freedom of speech was desirable because it would lead to the discovery of the truth. While all of the instrumental theories derive from Mill's philosophy, there is also a crossover and Mill also provided theoretical support for theories within the constitutive justification. To minimise confusion, Tedford and Herbeck divided the free speech theories as being philosophical, political or individual.[5] While not perfect, it probably furnishes a clearer division among free speech theories and, under this division, Mill's contribution falls within the philosophical reasons and the specific applications such as democracy theory fall within the political reason. In the twentieth century, the truth theory found modern expression in the marketplace of ideas theory as propounded by Justices Oliver Wendell Holmes and Louis Brandeis. Basically, the marketplace of ideas contemplated that people would make better choices and sounder decisions if debate were free and open. While this is less absolutist than Mill's concept of free speech leading to the discovery of truth, the marketplace of ideas is still geared toward idealistic belief in sound decisions and good choices. These concepts do not seem to find expression in the sociological needs for consensus through discourse. However, the relevance of Mill's truth theory to sociology takes a positive turn when some of the more modern criticisms of the truth theory are examined.

Frederick Schauer questioned whether the marketplace of ideas was more likely to lead to error or folly than to truth.[6] Schauer argued that the open exchange of ideas is more about consensus building than it is a test of truth and that consensus building has very little to do with the truth nor does it mean that truth will be accepted above folly. While these observations refute Mill's idealism, Schauer is squarely on point with why Habermas argued for freedom of expression from a sociological viewpoint. Habermas was concerned with building consensus or harmony in differentiated, multicultural modern society; truth is not relevant to the sociological ends. However, a key aspect of discourse theory is that each individual is treated with dignity and is entitled to be listened to and to have ideas taken seriously by other listeners. In the modern world of concentrated media ownership, it is difficult to argue that each speaker is given equal dignity. Mill did not directly address the ability of powerful people to dominate communication and the need for corrective measures to assure everyone the right to be heard. Habermas regarded informal settings such as coffee houses or discussion groups as the avenue for everyone to be heard. Conversely, efforts to afford equal access to competing editorial viewpoints have been ruled unconstitutional in the United States. Society requires consensus and according to Schauer's criticism of Mill's theory, consensus is the likely result of freedom of expression. Through this route, the sociology of freedom of speech reflected John Stuart Mill's philosophy as modernised by Frederick Schauer.

An instrumental theory that has found substantial legislative sanction in many countries is the democracy and self-government theory. Alexander Meiklejohn proposed that speech relating to self-government or democracy needed to be free for the democratic decision-making process to be effective. This theory fits well within Durkheim's concept of organic solidarity wherein members of society have become sufficiently individualised that there are many different beliefs and opinions. Since everyone does not share the same thoughts, collective action by government requires reaching consensus. To reach consensus, the members of society must communicate and based on Schauer's criticism of Mill as well as Habermas's sociology, freedom of expression is effective at building consensus.

Turning from the traditional results-oriented instrumental justification, the individual-oriented constitutive justification finds substantial application to society at large. In sociological terms, it is not difficult to see how freedom of expression enhances the lifeworld inhabited by individuals. Philosophers have developed numerous sound arguments how freedom of expression is an essential element of liberty, autonomy, dignity, and self-fulfilment. Those arguments stand and fall on their own merits. But, as applied to society as a whole, new territory is being explored. It is not enough to say that what is good for each individual is good for society because that is not necessarily true. Not paying taxes may be highly desirable for an individual but for society as a whole, it would be calamitous.

To the extent that philosophers establish that freedom of expression is essential for autonomy and individuation, then freedom of speech plays a key role in the effective functioning of societies dominated by organic solidarity. Just as free speech promotes individuation in complex society, it also provides the mechanism for coordinating and harmonising the activities of the individuals and this is where Habermas argued that freedom of expression is essential.

Thomas Scanlon proposed that freedom of speech was essential for individual sovereignty which he viewed as freedom to listen to available choices. Similarly C. Edwin Baker theorised that freedom of expression was essential for individual liberty. He held that under this concept, known as the liberty theory, expression was not a means to an end but an end unto itself and was intensely personal. However, sociologically, the liberty theory is a means to a necessary result. For organic solidarity to flourish, the individuals must possess autonomy based on their relative positions in complex society. Freedom of expression is not just desirable as a human value but is essential where division of labour exists and consensus must be reached in the absence of shared values. Interestingly, this argument may also be extended to the self-fulfilment theory which, on its face, eschews societal interests. Under this theory, freedom of speech belongs to each individual as a matter of self-gratification regardless of societal interests. Consequently, quite logically, Schauer maintained that self-fulfilment theory is individual and does not focus on the state or society.[7] Yet, from the viewpoint of organic solidarity, this is most certainly a societal interest because individuation is an essential aspect of the social division of labour. It is also essential to recognise that these individual reasons are not being usurped by sociology simply because they play a role in reaching consensus.

The point is more basic—organic solidarity absolutely requires that individuals occupying different roles in society be permitted to develop their own individualised perspectives and that this right is not simply individual but is societal as it is an essential aspect of the division of labour that is the defining feature of complex society.

At this point, the arguments almost become circular—philosophical arguments that support the individual's right to freedom of expression are not just beneficial to the individual but are also essential to the overall society or system. Because modern complex societies are based upon ever-more complex divisions of labour, individuals will possess increasingly disparate beliefs. In short, as division of labour increases, individual perspectives on just about everything diverge with the result that shared beliefs (commonplace where mechanical solidarity prevails) become increasingly rare. Without legally sanctioned individuation, division of labour is inhibited and the laws will be out of synch with social requirements. Beyond the societal need for individuation, in an environment where community agreement is not obvious, discourse is essential to find consensus so that the community can work, the constituent elements of society must communicate or very little can be achieved other than anarchy and constant conflict, a socially mediated entropic doom of sorts.

From the standpoint of economics, the division of labour creates an endless parade of increasingly specialised citizens each performing discrete functions requiring broad rights of communication. As government becomes more diffused and spread across innumerable boards, commissions, and agencies, compliance and regulation become increasingly challenging and require greater rights of communication between citizens and public authority. In countries with democratic governments at various levels, extensive discourse is needed to achieve consensus at every level. In more homogeneous societies, there may be more shared values than in more heterogeneous groups; in which case, the need for discourse is reduced with respect to the shared values. Consequently, the need for freedom of expression will differ among societies based on the extent that shared values may predominate. So, from a sociological standpoint, freedom of speech is essential for individuals to effectively function in complex societies but that freedom can be moderated to the extent that shared values exist.

Now, to where do these arguments lead? What is the point? The application of sociological theory was introduced to suggest that regardless of whether a freedom of expression theory has been categorised as falling within the instrumental or constitutive justification, virtually all of the traditional free speech theories support the free speech required by complex societies to function. In that very real sense, all of the free expression theories are instrumental—they assist in the smooth operation of societies typified by organic solidarity by promoting autonomy. In this respect, Durkheim's view of sociology was correct—it is at the apex absorbing specific theories contributed by other disciplines in an attempt to define the human social condition. There is substantial merit to all of the traditional free speech theories yet; ultimately, their real-world application is defined by their application to supporting division of labour inherent in modern complex and differentiated societies.

This leads to the final point—why is sociological transformation of constitutive theory into instrumental theory significant? Historically, courts, such as the US Supreme Court in *New York Times v. Sullivan* or the House of Lords in *Reynolds v. Times Newspapers*, have relied on instrumental free speech theory. Because the philosophical and individual reasons for freedom of expression have generally been cast in the constitutive lot, they are by definition not so much functional as more metaphysically desirable. This is not the stuff on which legislation or judicial decisions are usually based. However, if sociological theory is accepted, it is fundamentally erroneous, or at least incomplete, to cast the philosophical and individual theories as anything but functional and essential to the well-being of modern society. And, if so recategorised, international human rights commissions, legislatures, parliaments, and courts should give the same recognition to liberty or self-fulfilment as is accorded to democracy or self-government as the basis for extending rights of freedom of expression.

Sociological theory expands our understanding of the functional role of freedom of speech. It follows that to avoid disharmony between law and values, then freedom of speech must be expanded. Sociology calls for the law to expand speech rights rather than contract rights and argues that Kant and C. E. Baker should have the same level of legal acceptance as Meiklejohn. The question then becomes to what extent are sociological arguments recognised by courts? To gain insight on this question, in the next chapter, the viability of sociological arguments in the US Supreme Court will be examined.

Endnotes

1. Traditional free speech theory is discussed at length in chapter 5 and the sociological discussion is contained in chapter 2. Unless specifically needed, references to primary sources are not repeated in this discussion but can be found in chapters 5 and 2 respectively.
2. Gerd Nollman, "Habermas, Jurgen" in George Ritzer (ed), *Encyclopedia of Social Theory*, vol. 1, 351.
3. James Gordon Finlayson, *Habermas—A Very Short Introduction*, 106.
4. See Jurgen Habermas, *The Theory of Communicative Action*, V. 1, 397.
5. Thomas Tedford & Dale Herbeck, *Freedom of Speech in the United States*, 432.
6. Frederick Schauer, *Free Speech: A Philosophical Enquiry,* 21–30.
7. Ibid., 48.

CHAPTER 7

SOCIOLOGY AS LEGAL ARGUMENT

THE AMERICAN EXPERIENCE

If the arguments presented in this book have been at all persuasive, then it will have been established that the social division of labour can justify freedom of expression independent of traditional legal philosophy. However, is this finding merely something of interest for scholarly discussion or might it find application in actual public policy? For example, would the US Supreme Court be receptive to argument built on sociological theory? If the answer is in the affirmative, the arguments discussed in the preceding chapters might be used in future First Amendment arguments. The prognosis is favourable. At least with respect to the US Supreme Court, sociological arguments have not only been received but have, from time to time, been the basis for some key decisions, including some of the First Amendment decisions. Indeed, application of sociology assists in making sense of some defamation decisions that are difficult to square with legal theory alone. While the Supreme Court has not openly considered sociological theory in the context of theoreticians such as Durkheim or Habermas, it has responded favourably to sociological information and considerations. It would appear that the next step is to argue theory itself.

SOCIOLOGY IN THE COURTS

In order to determine the proper role of sociology in the legal system, it is useful to have working definitions of both sociology and law because the two are closely related. Professor Cotterrell provided a clear statement of the two concepts. "Law is a practical craft of systematic control of social relations and institutions. Sociology is the scientific enterprise that seeks systematic knowledge of them."[1] And, sociological theory has been defined as "a set of interrelated ideas that allows for the systemisation of knowledge of the social world, the explanation of that world, and predictions about the future of the social world."[2] In other words, law is the set of rules that control social relations whereas sociology is the science of understanding social relations and, sociological theory explains and predicts social conduct and therefore, should be useful in creating legal policy. In this respect, the relationship between laws and cultural values addressed in the Hart-Devlin disintegration thesis debate discussed in chapter 2 is relevant.

The distinction between sociology and sociological theory may appear significant to this discussion because while there are frequent situations where sociological information or sociology is relied upon by the Supreme Court, actual citation to sociological theory appears non-existent. However, this does not diminish the practical use of sociological theory because the Court does not always acknowledge legal theory even when the Court's opinion is directly derived from that theory. Perhaps the most salient example of this is the seminal First Amendment decision of *New York Times v. Sullivan* in which Justice Brennan, writing for the Court, relied extensively on the democracy free speech theory espoused earlier by Professor Alexander Meiklejohn and never once even acknowledged Meiklejohn's contribution or, for that matter, Meiklejohn's existence. Yet, it can be reasonably assumed that Justice Brennan had Meiklejohn in mind when the decision was written because, one year later, in a paper delivered at Brown University at the rather aptly named Alexander Meiklejohn Lecture, Justice Brennan said of *New York Times v. Sullivan*:

"the case presented a classic example of an activity that Dr. Meiklejohn called an activity of 'governing importance' within the powers reserved to the people and made invulnerable to sanctions imposed by their agency-governments."[3] While the failure to acknowledge Professor Meiklejohn in *New York Times v. Sullivan* was likely just an oversight, the significance of the point is simply that failure to cite explicitly the theory by name does not diminish the role of theory in the judicial decision-making process. The ultimate issue is whether sociology can constitute legitimate argument for First Amendment interpretation regardless of acknowledgement in the Court's decision.

In point of fact, it is not difficult to find sociology sometimes being more persuasive than legal arguments in Supreme Court decision making. Sociology is a very broad discipline that has as its goal the organisation and understanding of social relations. The theory is just one step beyond—providing the underlying reason why social systems behave in the manner they exhibit. As in all sciences, theory is vindicated when it actually has predictive value. Before looking at the role of sociology in First Amendment matters, it is useful to look at some familiar situations in which the court has not hesitated to go outside the legal realm and instead based its decisions on sociological information.

One of the most far-reaching decisions of the post–World War II court was *Brown v. Board of Education.*[4] In this decision, the Supreme Court held that the long-established tradition of separate schooling for African American children in the southern states simply could not stand. The argument in favour of the existing structure was the long-held belief that as long as the schooling was "equal," that there was no constitutional problem. Writing for the Court, Chief Justice Warren relied on argument that was clearly more at home in a sociology text than in a law book:

> In *Sweatt v. Painter,* in finding that a segregated law school for Negroes could not provide them equal educational opportunities, this Court relied in large part on 'those qualities which are incapable of objective measurement but which make for greatness in

> a law school.' In *McLaurin v. Oklahoma*, the Court, in requiring that a Negro admitted to a white graduate school be treated like all other students, again resorted to intangible considerations: '*** his ability to study, to engage in discussions and exchange views with other students, and, in general, to learn his profession.' Such considerations apply with added force to children in grade and high schools. To separate them from others of similar age and qualifications solely because of their race generates a feeling of inferiority as to their status in the community that may affect their hearts and minds in a way unlikely ever to be undone.[5]

In *Brown v. Board of Education,* the court instituted broad changes through the equal protection clause of the Fourteenth Amendment by giving judicial sanction to social relations and institutions, namely, the harm to children's self-esteem caused by separation on the sole grounds of race. Sociological argument effectively carried the day.

Sociology played a key role in another well-known case, *Miranda v. Arizona*, which was decided in 1966.[6] Writing for a majority, Chief Justice Warren stated that persons detained because of suspected criminal conduct had to be given explicit warning that any statements made by them could be used against them and that they had a right to counsel. Arguably, this was merely stating the obvious as both requirements are relatively clear in the Fifth and Sixth Amendments. But, the Chief Justice went beyond this and laid down the very controversial principle that has become known as the exclusionary rule: "unless and until such warnings and waiver are demonstrated by the prosecution at trial, no evidence obtained as a result of interrogation can be used against him."[7] Anticipating strong objections from state governments and local prosecutors, the court wrote to the Solicitor General and requested Federal Bureau of Investigation (FBI) data that detailed both procedures and experiences relating to giving the warnings already required of federal prosecutors. The Court found the FBI experience convincing.[8] Again, empirical social data was employed to establish constitutional principles.

Perhaps nowhere in constitutional law is sociology as useful as its application in defamation law. From the basis of legal and philosophical free speech theory alone, it is well-nigh impossible to understand the hodgepodge of rules found in modern American defamation law. As was shown in chapter 5, free speech theory is very much content driven. Most clearly, Meiklejohn's democracy theory that advocates freedom of speech relating to democratic government clearly demands that defamation law not restrain speech relating to public matters. Yet, except for a brief period of only three years, American First Amendment interpretations have never focused on content but rather have looked to the identity of the target of the speech to determine if the speech should be protected. From the viewpoint of legal theory, the Supreme Court decisions are quite unsatisfying and are disconnected from sound reasoning. Yet, if sociological considerations are added to the mix, the American hodgepodge becomes much more logical and well-reasoned. If this is the case, the constitutional door should be wide open for free speech arguments that openly sound in social theory. So, while sociological theory has never been directly employed in free speech arguments, the fact that social factors have played a significant role in decision-making makes sociological argument all the more appealing inasmuch as the concept is not alien to the court's practices.

In the *New York Times v. Sullivan* decision, the US Supreme Court elected to protect many otherwise defamatory publications about the conduct of public officials unless the publication was made with actual knowledge of falsity or with reckless disregard of the truth. Given that most activities of public officials have a bearing on their fitness for or actual performance of pubic duties, it can be argued that the court's decision was not so far off as to be a real departure from Meiklejohn's content based democracy theory. But it was with the subsequent decisions in *Garrison v. Louisiana*[9] and *Curtis Publishing Co. v. Butts*[10] that sociology seems to play a greater role than legal theory. In *Garrison,* discussed at length in chapter 3, the Supreme Court rather overtly made social—as opposed to legal—arguments with respect to the inappropriateness of criminal defamation in modern society. Justice Brennan wrote:

> Changing mores and the virtual disappearance of criminal libel prosecutions lend support to the observation that…under modern conditions, when the rule of law is generally accepted as a substitute for private physical measures, it can hardly be urged that the maintenance of peace requires a criminal prosecution for private defamation.[11]

Although Emile Durkheim's theoretical contribution was not recognised (similar to Meiklejohn not being mentioned in *New York Times*), the court's opinion rests solidly on Durkheim's theory about the evolution of law from criminal to restitutionary as division of labour in society increases and shared values tend to decrease. Perhaps this is the clearest case for the legitimacy of sociological theory in Supreme Court argument because the court's conclusion fits squarely within social theory though no one acknowledged it as such at the time.

In *Curtis Publishing*, the claimant was not a public official and the speech at issue had to do with alleged fixing of college football games and not with a matter concerning government or elected officials. Yet, the court extended First Amendment protections to defamatory statements made concerning public figures, such as celebrities or athletes or anyone else who is well-known. In his concurring opinion, Chief Justice Warren wrote:

> To me, differentiation between 'public figures' and 'public officials' and adoption of separate standards of proof for each have no basis in law, logic, or First Amendment policy. Increasingly in this country, the distinctions between governmental and private sectors are blurred. Since the depression of the 1930's and World War II there has been a rapid fusion of economic and political power, a merging of science, industry, and government, and a high degree of interaction between the intellectual, governmental, and business worlds. Depression, war, international tensions, national and international markets, and the surging growth of science and technology have precipitated national and international problems that demand national and international solutions….This blending of positions

> and power has also occurred in the case of individuals so that many who do not hold public office at the moment are nevertheless intimately involved in the resolution of important public questions or, by reason of their fame, shape events in areas of concern to society at large.[12]

Chief Justice Warren was performing an exercise that falls very appropriately within sociology; he was attempting to explain a condition found in modern society, namely, the blurring of public and private worlds with the result that public opinion was as much the product of private as well as public figures. His comments about the fusion of economic and government power predate but sound like Habermas's concept of system and its concomitant influence on the lifeworld inhabited by citizens.

The Chief Justice concluded that no distinction should be made in the legal treatment of public person claimants regardless of whether they are employed within the public or private sectors because of the influence they exert on the public. This certainly goes beyond Meiklejohn's theoretical framework because it reaches far beyond political decision because once accorded public figure status, the defamation privilege applies regardless of context. Consequently if the criticism of the public figure is directed toward matters of fashion, the speech would still be protected. In a content directed theory of freedom of speech, protected expression would not extend to such matters. Indeed, in the United Kingdom where a content-oriented freedom of speech privilege applies, popularly known as the *Reynolds* defence or reasonable journalism, talk about taste in clothes or marital escapades would likely fall outside the zone of protected speech. As observed by Baroness Hale in *Jameel v. Wall Street Journal (Europe)*:

> There must be a real public interest in communicating and receiving the information. This is, as we all know, very different from saying that it is information which interests the public, the most vapid tittle-tattle about footballers' wives and girlfriends invites large sections of the public but no-one could claim any real public interest in our being told about it.[13]

In the context of traditional free speech theory, Baroness Hale is undoubtedly correct. But, with the substitution or addition of sociologic theory, especially Habermas's conception of system intruding on lifeworld, the broader Warren formulation has much to commend it. Habermas was concerned with the ability of the governing power structure, whether it be economic or governmental, to displace or even destroy the lifeworld by channelling behaviour contrary to the best interests of the citizens.[14] The American approach of allowing free speech to challenge any aspect of the public figure provides an outlet by which the lifeworld can respond to challenges by the governing power structure or system.

The Chief Justice also articulated another argument for extending the scope of the First Amendment to speech concerning public officials that appears to be far more sociological than legal. He stated that public persons should be treated as public officials because public persons "have as ready access as 'public officials' to mass media of communication, both to influence policy and to counter criticism of their views and activities."[15] While ability to respond seems like a reasonable concept, it does not lend itself to any of the traditional legal theories.

In 1971, just four years after the *Curtis Publishing* decision, the Supreme Court, in a radical departure from the public figure and public official concept, announced that the constitutional defamation privilege would hinge on content rather than the public status of the claimant. In *Rosenbloom v. Metromedia,* the plurality decision by Justice Brennan was only joined by two other members of the Court, with two others joining only in the result.[16] Justice Brennan wrote that the defamation privilege expanding freedom of expression would attach in all cases where the subject matter of the speech was a matter of public concern regardless of the status of the complainant.[17] *Rosenbloom*, focusing on speech content, was much more in line with speech theory, especially as proposed by Meiklejohn than were the earlier decisions. But, *Rosenbloom* only lasted three years. In 1974, *Gertz v. Robert Welch, Inc.*, reversed *Rosenbloom* and reinstated the defamation privilege based on public person status as opposed to speech content.[18] In *Gertz,* the Supreme Court recognised a new class of public person known as the limited-purpose public figure and, as applied to this class of persons, the broad defamation privilege would only attach if there was a matter of public controversy or interest and the limited-purpose figure was connected with that subject matter.

After creating the limited-purpose public figure, in subsequent cases, the Supreme Court proceeded to cobble together numerous permutations of the basic defamation privilege in an effort to accommodate various factual situations. For example, in *Philadelphia Newspapers, Inc. v. Hepps,* the court held that there would be some level of First Amendment protection even though the target of the speech was a private figure. This was based on the factual circumstance that the subject matter was of public interest and the publisher was the media.[19] Again, this conclusion is difficult to square with legal theory alone but if sociologic facts are considered, the decision is rather sensible. Writing for a deeply divided court, Justice Sandra Day O'Connor stated that the Court's finding was limited to the situation involving a private person plaintiff, a media publisher, and speech where the subject matter is of public interest. The decision did not reach the question of whether the same privilege would apply to a publisher who was not a member of the media.[20] In his concurring opinion, Justice Brennan did not subscribe to the court's failure to extend the ruling to cases where the publisher was not a member of the media.[21]

In *Philadelphia Newspapers,* Justice Brennan was refusing to distinguish between classes of defendants as he saw the right of free speech attaching regardless of the status of the publisher. This generally squares with legal theory because it also does not distinguish among speakers to determine legal rights. Yet, Justice O'Connor's opinion recognised the special status and role of the media in society to write about controversial topics and the court was clearly trying to give the media some extra breathing room. Again, a factor, more sociological than legal, plays a central role in the court's decision making.

Despite this long record of interposing sociological information as the basis for legal principles, the practice is not without its critics. For example, in the 2011 Supreme Court decision *Sykes v. United States*, in his dissent, Justice Scalia referred to the Court's "tutti-fruitti opinion" based on what he perceived to be dubious statistical evidence.[22] *Sykes* required the Supreme Court to interpret the meaning of a statute that provided for enhanced incarceration of persons convicted of a felony who had three prior convictions of a violent felony. In the case of Mr Sykes, he had a prior conviction for using a motor vehicle for escape from a law enforcement officer. The question before the court was whether flight by motor vehicle constituted a "violent felony" which the statute described as something that "presents a serious potential risk of physical injury to another."[23] Justice Scalia was all for declaring the statute void for vagueness but a majority of six disagreed and, citing substantial statistical information that was contained in the government's papers, the court held that escape by way of a motor vehicle constituted a violent felony. The heart of Justice Scalia's argument was that the holding was not based on actual evidence but on sociological studies concerning risk of injury and historical results of escapes by motor vehicle. His complaint was that there was but a tutti-fruitti presentation in which studies were accepted on faith "without examining their methodology at all."[24]

`While the "tutti-fruitti" reference seems to be that of a hard-nosed judge rejecting soft sociological data as inappropriate for a court to use in decision making, Justice Scalia's comments could simply refer to the quality of the presentation that had been made in this particular case. While "tutti fruitti" in this context is both disparaging and humorous, Justice Scalia makes special mention of the fact that the studies had never been introduced into evidence at the lower courts and were merely cited in appeal papers without any showing of the scientific validity of the studies. To this end, he pointed out diverging results among the studies and, in essence, questioned reliability rather than relevance. Notwithstanding Justice Scalia's reservations, the court accepted the use of the sociological data to help fashion rules of law or interpretations of law.

Recognising that the US Supreme Court does not hesitate to inject sociology into its proceedings despite the "tutti-fruitti" implications, how far can it be from recognising the validity of sociological theory as the basis for decision making? There would not seem to be any obstacle to arguing theory as long as the factual support is also presented. For example, in *Brown v. Board of Education,* the court recognised that as a factual matter, separate could never be equal because of the effect separate status would have on the psyche of schoolchildren. Even if the school physical plants were identical, separate simply could not be equal. This finding is not only supported by studies but it is likely also be supported by sound social theory. The value of theory, in addition to statistical or data intensive studies, is that sound application of theory can eliminate or reduce the risk that data alone amounts to tutti-frutti evidence. Data consistent with theory not only validates the theory but also helps to sustain the interpretation of the data itself—data and theory are mutually supportive. Theory can help to fashion broad doctrine with the assurance that the doctrine is moving in the correct direction. Application of Habermas's and Durkheim's theories as the basis for broad communicative rights can provide benchmarks for assuring that a specific, proposed expanded speech right is helpful to society.

Sociological theory is meant to explain human conduct in the context of society as opposed to individuals. Law is meant to govern relations among individuals in society. To the extent that sociological theory can inform the courts and law makers about social behaviour and social expectations, the law will more correctly reflect social needs. Sociological theory is a helpful tool that can assist the courts to assure that laws both reflect social values and work toward social goals. Indeed, as discussed in the following section, it is sociology that helps rescue the US Supreme Court from the sometimes eccentric language of the American legal framework.

THE AMERICAN CONUNDRUM

A conundrum is a puzzle, and it is indeed puzzling to attempt to unravel the difficulty of balancing freedom of expression and other legitimate interests within the confines of the American First Amendment. While freedom of expression is always featured prominently in modern human rights charters or bills of rights, the freedom is explicitly balanced against other interests. Article 10 of the *European Convention on Human Rights* provides for a right of expression but also recognises competing interests such as reputation, social order and dignity. The goal of achieving balance invites application of sociological factors. The eighteenth-century American First Amendment recognises no such balance—on its face, it is an all-or-nothing proposition. While the Europeans may or may not find a correct balancing of interests, the Americans have to struggle even to find the authority to balance interests. Yet, the US Supreme Court has imposed a balance. This section discusses some of the challenges faced by the Supreme Court in this effort.

Perhaps some people would argue that freedom of expression is so important that it must trump all other interests all of the time. Yet, this has never been the accepted view. American state and federal laws regulate expression in numerous areas such as broadcasting, child pornography, and even defamation and privacy law. However, all of these regulations on speech are challenged by the First Amendment. The painful legal and legislative history of campaign finance reform bears testimony to how the First Amendment with its literal absolutes helps to entrench well-funded politicians. While a solution to the conundrum is not apparent, the cause and history of the situation is not nearly so elusive. Enabled by the Fourteenth Amendment and in the context of serious social issues, the twentieth-century US Supreme Court has creatively utilised the eighteenth-century First Amendment to provide solutions to twentieth- and twenty-first-century problems. But, when the square peg is jammed into the round hole, there are bound to be consequences and they are convoluted, tortuous, and frequently intellectually unsatisfying without recourse to some concept beyond black-letter law and legal theory.

In the preface, former US Supreme Court Justice Arthur Goldberg was quoted for his observation in *Kennedy v. Mendoza-Martinez* that the US Constitution is not a suicide pact. While it may not attain the status of being a suicide pact, the First Amendment guarantees of freedom of speech contained in the words "Congress shall make no law…abridging the freedom of speech" do not permit a great deal of flexibility in interpretation or balance among various countervailing social interests such as privacy or equal access for opposing opinions. While Justice Black's interpretation of the First Amendment, contained in his concurring opinion in *New York Times v. Sullivan,* that the First Amendment is an absolute and that there can be no restrictions whatsoever on the press, has never attracted a majority of the Supreme Court; his interpretation is not all that far off the mark. The simple truth is that the plain text of the First Amendment contains the words "Congress shall make no law" and on its face this does not permit much give and take. If the Founders did not intend to give the press free rein to publish known falsehoods, what was Madison thinking when he drafted the First Amendment? The answer can be found in the chequered interpretation of the First Amendment itself.

It is not difficult to find examples where Supreme Court interpretations of the First Amendment seem to counter sound free speech theory with the result that the First Amendment works to stifle rather than promote the marketplace of ideas or the search for truth. One of the methods proposed for equalisation of the marketplace of ideas in political contests is the concept of economic regulation of campaign expenditures by candidates on their own campaigns.[25] However, the US Supreme Court has found that many aspects of guaranteeing equal access constitute either coerced speech or unconstitutional limits on free speech. In *Buckley v. Valeo,* while upholding many aspects of campaign finance reform, the US Supreme Court struck down, as violating the First Amendment, restrictions on the amount candidates could contribute to their own campaigns.[26]

While couching their opinion in First Amendment terms, this was a classic situation where the court grounded its reasoning on social reality as opposed to an idealised concept. As a practical matter, candidates who are known to be wealthy sometimes have insurmountable difficulty as public fundraisers. This decision was handed down while Nelson Rockefeller was vice president of the United States and his experiences of self-funding campaigns over the course of a long political history both as state and national candidate would have been obvious and well known to the justices. Today, the situation of New York Mayor Michael Bloomberg would also be a case in point.

In another example, a Florida law that guaranteed a right of reply to newspaper editorials was held to constitute coerced speech in *Miami Herald Publishing Co v. Tornillo*[27] and certain laws restricting corporate campaign expenditures have been stricken as impermissible restrictions on free speech in the 2010 Supreme Court decision *Citizens United v. Federal Election Commission.*[28] Compelling arguments have been made that First Amendment interpretations such as those found in *Miami Herald* and *Citizens United* do not support democracy and truth but, rather, undermine it because they fail to recognise the need for political equality.[29] This is an instance where doctrinal law fails to recognise the underlying theoretical reasoning regarding freedom of expression with the consequence that the First Amendment ultimately yields an illogical result. Instead of promoting Mill's goals of providing citizens with information so that the best collective decision can be reached, these interpretations of the First Amendment can achieve just the opposite by permitting speech to be distorted in favour of the party with the largest resources or greatest access to the media.[30] Contrary to First Amendment jurisprudence, a logical argument can be made that there is a legitimate role for the state in preserving freedom of speech and that it is incorrect to only think of government as an antagonist to free speech.[31] From a sociological standpoint, Durkheim and Habermas also saw an important role for the state in maintaining the framework that permitted democratic society to function. In his evaluation of whether *New York Times* should be transplanted into Australian law,

Professor Michael Chesterman took special note of the anomaly produced by the *Miami Herald* case. While supposedly embracing the marketplace of ideas or self-government theories, the US Supreme Court, in its preoccupation with abstaining from state-controlled content regulation, blocked an otherwise content-neutral effort to improve public debate.[32]

American courts have so doggedly pursued a rigid policy about keeping government out of content regulation that opportunities for enhancing public debate and the discovery of truth have been lost when they could have been publicly nurtured. For example, the Florida statute guaranteeing a right of reply to newspaper editorials for political candidates that was held to be unconstitutional in the *Miami Herald* decision was intended to assure that both sides of political debate would be heard.[33] Yet, the Supreme Court refused to engage in evaluating the merits of the legislation but rather peremptorily dismissed the free speech arguments that supported the statute on the grounds that government must not be involved in content regulation.[34] Similarly, in 2008, the Supreme Court held that a portion of the *McCain-Feingold Campaign Finance Law of 2002* was unconstitutional because it sought to help equalise financial resources of congressional candidates.[35] The statute sought to promote free speech by permitting larger campaign contributions to candidates in situations where their opponents spent over $350,000 of their personal funds on their campaign. The intent of the statute was to better assure that the messages of both candidates would be heard by the electorate. Nevertheless, the Supreme Court held that the law was incompatible with the First Amendment because it imposed a penalty on wealthy candidates who desired to exercise robustly their free speech rights. The court, in a 5-4 decision, felt that attempts to influence, let alone to equalise, campaign presentations to the public had "ominous implications."[36] While ostensibly authorised by the First Amendment, it can certainly be argued that the court's decision did not promote any recognised free speech theory except for the mistrust of government.

To attempt an explanation for the inflexibility of the First Amendment requires some examination of the historical record. When adopted, the First Amendment did not apply to the states but was limited to the federal government. Consequently, the states were free to regulate speech and balance interests as they sought fit. When the First Amendment was initially proposed, Madison considered making it binding on the states. However, he backed away from this proposal because of the conflict of the freedom of religion clause and the reality that several states, namely Connecticut and Massachusetts, still had state churches. Consequently, the First Amendment guaranteed rights only with respect to the federal government and, the reference to "Congress shall make no law" meant just that—the restriction was on the federal legislature and the guarantee did not have any application to the conduct of the individual States.

Significantly, the State Constitutions, while guaranteeing a right to expression also acknowledged restrictions on the right—restrictions which are unknown to the First Amendment.[37] A few comparisons in the following examples make the point (emphasis added).

> **US First Amendment:** "Congress shall make no law…abridging the freedom of speech, or of the press…."
>
> **Alabama:** "That no law shall ever be passed to curtail or restrain the liberty of speech or of the press; and any person may speak, write, and publish his sentiments on all subjects, *being responsible for the abuse of that liberty.*[38]
>
> **California:** Every person may freely speak, write and publish his or her sentiments on all subjects, *being responsible for the abuse of this right."*[39]
>
> **Connecticut:** "Every citizen may freely speak, write and publish his sentiments on all subjects *being responsible for the abuse of that liberty."*[40]

> **Florida:** "Every person may speak, write and publish sentiments on all subjects *but shall be responsible for the abuse of that right*."[41]
>
> **New York:** "Every citizen may freely speak, write and publish his or her sentiments on all subjects, *being responsible for the abuse of that right*; and no law shall be passed to restrain or abridge the liberty of speech or of the press."[42]
>
> **Texas:** "Every person shall be at liberty to speak, write or publish his opinions on any subject, *being responsible for the abuse of that privilege*; and no law shall ever be passed curtailing the liberty of speech or of the press."[43]
>
> **Wyoming:** "Every person may freely speak, write and publish on all subjects, *being responsible for the abuse of that right....*"[44]

While there are variations among the language used by the states, invariably there is mention of liability attaching in the event of abuse of the right, and the right to speak is stated affirmatively not as a negative statement prohibiting government regulation as is found in the First Amendment. The state concept of personal liability attaching if the right is abused is not paralleled in the federal constitution.[45] Under the state constitutions, defamation law grew along lines closely following traditional common law principles.

Given that it only applied to the activities of the federal government toward citizens, the First Amendment was traditionally of limited application and did not affect regulation of speech by the States and, within the confines of their own constitutions, the States were free to balance rights of free speech as they deemed appropriate. However, in a series of twentieth-century Supreme Court decisions, the federal-state dynamic was to change dramatically and the First Amendment, with its seeming absolute prohibition of laws regulating speech, was to eclipse the state constitutions. The Supreme Court decisions may not have been intended to disturb the balance between state and federal rights but that was the inevitable consequence. Again, history comes into play.

More than half a century after the adoption of the Bill of Rights, the Fourteenth Amendment was ratified in the aftermath of the US Civil War in an effort to keep the former states of the Confederacy from denying basic human rights to African American citizens. Again, another half century was to pass before the Fourteenth Amendment began its evolution or more properly, metamorphosis into the most potent alteration to the US Constitution since the adoption of the Bill of Rights. In modern interpretations, the Fourteenth Amendment has transformed the Bill of Rights from merely regulating federal conduct to a body of law regulating government at all levels. This metamorphosis, which has very broad implications for the balance between freedom of expression and other interests, had a rather inauspicious birth in the 1925 Supreme Court case of *Gitlow v. New York*.[46] In this case, Benjamin Gitlow had been convicted of the crime of criminal anarchy by the state of New York. Gitlow had been distributing publications of the Left Wing Section of the Socialist Party that urged that the proletariat needed to take matters into their own hands and achieve a communist revolution through militant and revolutionary socialism without recourse to the ballot box. Gitlow was tried and convicted of advocating the overthrow of the government through violent means. The fact that the incitement did not result in any violence or unlawful activity was not a factor in the offence. The Supreme Court affirmed the conviction with Justices Holmes and Brandeis dissenting. Holmes and Brandeis were of the opinion, later to become law, that without any present danger of violence, the words of incitement were nothing more than enthusiastic opinion. Holmes wrote:

> The only difference between the expression of an opinion and an incitement in the narrower sense is the speaker's enthusiasm for the result. Eloquence may set fire to reason. But whatever may be thought of the redundant discourse before us it had no chance of starting a present conflagration. If in the long run the beliefs expressed in the proletariat dictatorship are destined to be accepted by the dominant forces of the community, the only meaning of free

> speech is that they should be given their chance and have their way.[47]

While affirming the conviction, despite the absence of any evidence of threatened violence, and perhaps as throwing the proverbial bone to its two most brilliant members, the majority of the Supreme Court acquiesced and assumed that the dissenters were correct that the Fourteenth Amendment's guarantee that no state would deprive its citizens of life, liberty, or property without due process of law made the First Amendment applicable to the states as well as the federal government. The majority acknowledged:

> For present purposes we may and do assume that freedom of speech and of the press, which are protected by the First Amendment from abridgment by Congress, are among the fundamental personal rights and "liberties" protected by the due process clause of the Fourteenth Amendment from impairment by the States.[48]

This statement altered the delicate balance among the states and federal governments in ways that continue to reverberate in American law. By 1925, the institution of state churches had long disappeared in the United States and there was not any obvious vested interest to vociferously object to this intrusion of the First Amendment into what had been the province of state law. Since Benjamin Gitlow's conviction was affirmed, the Court's conclusion that the First Amendment was binding on the states did not have immediate impact. Forty years later, however, the precedent set by *Gitlow v. New York* was to change defamation law and freedom of speech in the United States forever.

The most recent chapter of First Amendment based federal-state relations arose from a libel suit that was initially erroneously decided by the state courts of Alabama. On March 29, 1960, the *New York Times* had published a full-page advertisement soliciting funds to aid in the civil rights struggle being led by Dr Martin Luther King. There were apparently several factual errors in the story that appear quite innocuous such as the report that students sang the national anthem on the state capital's steps when in fact they sang "My Country Tis of Thee." No one was specifically named as the perpetrator of offences against the civil rights workers except for references to "police" and "Southern violators." A relative handful of the newspapers were distributed in the State of Alabama. From these rather modest facts emerged the landmark decision of *New York Times v. Sullivan.*[49]

One of the key elements that a plaintiff must establish to prevail in a defamation action is that the publication was of and concerning the plaintiff. The plaintiff, L.B. Sullivan, was not mentioned at all in the article. However, he served as police commissioner and alleged that references to police misconduct defamed him. Under normal circumstances, plaintiff's case should never have reached the jury and should have been dismissed. But these were hardly normal circumstances; this was the time of the great Civil Rights Movement of the 1960s and local tempers were high. There was a great deal of anger in the South directed not just against citizens demanding their human rights but there was also some not altogether unjustified resentment toward northern (New York City) self-righteous indignation that was believed to be tinged with hypocrisy. In this environment, the state courts and juries in Alabama were unlikely to offer neutral tribunals.

The jury decision was ultimately affirmed by the Supreme Court of Alabama and, under the US Constitution, it was there that the matter would normally have terminated. Unlike other federations like Australia, the high court of the United States is generally precluded from reviewing common law decisions of the state supreme courts. The result is that there is not a unified common law in the United States but fifty separate bodies of law, each under the review of a state supreme court. However, it was recognised that the stakes were simply too high to permit Sullivan's victory to stand. He had received a verdict in his favour of $500,000 and the threat of future verdicts could very well have deterred national media from reporting the unhappy events taking place in the South.

After losing at the Supreme Court of Alabama, the *New York Times* petitioned the US Supreme Court to review the matter. Under the US Constitution, the Supreme Court only had jurisdiction to review federal constitutional issues. Consequently, the Supreme Court was required to leave undisturbed all of the common law errors made by the trial court and compounded by the Alabama Supreme Court. While the obvious grounds for reversal was failure of proof—the article not being of and concerning the plaintiff—the US Supreme Court could only intervene to the extent allowed by federal issues. Defamation law had always been a state matter but the Supreme Court was able to assert jurisdiction because of First Amendment issues, courtesy of *Gitlow v. New York*.

The US Supreme Court relied on the First and Fourteenth Amendments and held that the rule of law, not the factual findings, relied on by the Alabama courts was constitutionally defective for not adequately protecting freedom of expression.[50] Writing for the court, Justice Brennan said:

> It is true that the First Amendment was originally addressed only to action by the Federal Government, and that Jefferson, for one, while denying the power of Congress 'to control the freedom of the press,' recognized such a power in the States. See the 1804 Letter to Abigail Adams quoted in *Denis v. United States*, 341 US 494, 522, n 4, 71 S Ct 857, 95 L Ed 1137 (concurring opinion). But this distinction was eliminated with the adoption of the Fourteenth Amendment and the application to the States of the First Amendment's restrictions. See, for example, *Gitlow v. New York*, 268 US 652,666.[51]

The court proceeded to conclude that the First Amendment required substantial changes to the common law with respect to defamation claims brought by public officials concerning their official conduct. From this spawned the Byzantine latticework of standards and burdens of proof that now comprises American defamation law. As stated by one US district court, "the Supreme Court has 'federalized' defamation law as it relates to public figures or issues of public concern…."[52]

As a direct result of this sequence of events, the United States incurs substantial angst in the effort to balance various human rights issues that continue to emerge. As designed and originally implemented, the US Constitution allows the states to balance expression with other interests such as human dignity and privacy. The state constitutions invariably balance the right of free expression with responsibility for abuse of that privilege. This is not unlike the terms of Article 10 of the European Convention of Human Rights that balances the right of free expression with restrictions "as are prescribed by and are necessary in a democratic society" and "for the protection of the reputation or rights of others…" But now, as a result of *Gitlow v. New York* and *New York Times v. Sullivan*, the United States has imposed, on all levels of government, restrictions that were written and designed to be directed only at the national government.

When ratified, the Founders did not intend the First Amendment to apply to the states as it would disrupt the religious affairs of at least several states. Those religious sensitivities have long vanished but new concerns have arisen such as hate speech, human dignity, media centralisation, and privacy. Had the First Amendment been interpreted as the Founders intended, the American states would have been free to legislate and respond to twenty-first century human rights issues. But that opportunity has been constrained by a series of decisions imposing the near or at least ostensible absoluteness of the First Amendment on all levels of American legislation. The First Amendment was never meant to be a suicide pact. Yet, from the perspective of modern human rights, the inflexibility and absoluteness of the First Amendment can challenge the freedom of the Supreme Court to find the correct balance among sometimes conflicting human rights. In this historical and legal context, sociological theory might play a role as one more tool available to the court as it grapples with contemporary challenges.

ENDNOTES

1. Roger Cotterrell, *The Sociology of Law*, 5.
2. George Ritzer, *Contemporary Social Theory & Its Classical Roots*, 5.
3. William J. Brennan, Jr., "The Supreme Court and the Meiklejohn Interpretation of the First Amendment", *Harvard University Law Review* 79 (1965): 1.
4. 347 U.S. 483 (1954).
5. Ibid., 493–494.
6. 384 U.S. 436 (1966).
7. Ibid., 479.
8. Ibid., 483–486.
9. 379 US 64 (1964).
10. 388 US 130 (1967).
11. 379 US 64, 69 (1964).
12. 388 U.S. 130, 163-164 (1967).
13. *Jameel v. Wall Street Journal (Europe)* [2007], 1 A.C. 359, 408 (H.L. 2007).
14. James Gordon Finlayson, *Habermas—A Very Short Introduction*, 56.
15. *Curtis Publishing v. Butts*, 388 US 130, 164.
16. 403 U.S. 29 (1971).
17. Ibid., 52.
18. 418 US 323 (1974).
19. 475 US 767 (1986).
20. Ibid., 779, fn 4.
21. Ibid., 780.
22. 131 Sup. Ct. 2267, 2285 (2011).
23. Ibid., 2284.
24. Ibid., 2286.
25. Mark Graber, *Transforming Free Speech: The Ambiguous Legacy of Civil Libertarianism*, 227–234.
26. 424 US 1 (1976).
27. *Miami Herald Publishing Co v. Tornillo,* 418 US 241 (1974) ('*Miami Herald*').
28. *Citizens United v. Federal Election* Commission, 558 US __, 130 S Ct 876 (2010) ('*Citizens United'*); *Buckley v. Valeo,* 424 US 1 (1976).
29. Cass Sunstein, *Democracy and the Problem of Free Speech*, 93–119.

30. Ibid.
31. Owen Fiss, *Liberalism Divided: Freedom of Speech and the Many Uses of State Power*, 13–26.
32. Michael Chesterman, "The Money or the Truth: Defamation Reform in Australia and the USA", *University of New South Wales Law Journal* 18 (1995): 300, 314-316.
33. Owen Fiss, *The Irony of Free Speech*, 82–83.
34. *Miami Herald,* 418 US 241 (1974).
35. *Davis v. Federal Election Commission*, 128 S Ct 2759 (2008).
36. Ibid., 2773–2774.
37. See Robert Williams, *The Law of American State Constitutions*, 116.
38. *Alabama Constitution of 1901*, Sec. 4.
39. *California Constitution,* Article 1, Sec. 2(a).
40. *Constitution of the State of Connecticut*, Article First, Sec. 4.
41. *Constitution of the State of Florida,* Article 1, Sec. 4.
42. *Constitution of the State of New York,* Article 1, Sec. 8.
43. *The Texas Constitution*, Article 1, Sec. 8.
44. *Wyoming Constitution,* Article 1, Sec. 20.
45. See e.g., *Pines v. Tomson,* 160 Cal App3d 370, 392 (1984).
46. 268 US 652 (1925)
47. Ibid., 673
48. Ibid., 666.
49. 376 US 254 (1964).
50. Ibid., 264.
51. Ibid., 276–277.
52. *Roffman v. Trump*, 754 F.Supp. 411, 415 (ED PA 1990).

Conclusion

The Contribution of Sociological Theory to Free Speech

For too long, freedom of speech has been approached as something only belonging to and benefitting individuals. The goal of this discussion has been to open a new perspective and establish that the most individualistic reasons for freedom of expression are essential for the well-being of modern complex societies, especially in modern industrialised democracies where shared and commonly held beliefs are in the minority as compared to individual perspectives. The sociological explanations offered were based on pioneering work by Emile Durkheim and more recent contributions by Jurgen Habermas. However, the validity of the arguments discussed in the preceding chapters does not entirely depend upon whether the reader accepts the theories espoused by these scholars. The more critical point is that social theory can independently support freedom of expression as well as explain some of the limitations of more well-established legal and philosophical theories.

Durkheim's concept of organic and mechanical solidarities offers a compelling explanation for why rights that have been traditionally held to be individual are, in fact, essentially societal rights. For social division of labour to operate successfully, individuation must be allowed to flourish. Individuation is the essential consequence of citizens playing different roles and having different perspectives. This must be contrasted with the more primitive situation where there is less division of labour, and shared values and thoughts predominate. It would be anomalous for laws to restrict individual expression where individuation must thrive. Given that individuation is the natural consequence or essential aspect of division of labour, then the law must accommodate freedom of expression or the law will be at odds with societal needs.

Habermas built on Durkheim's work by directly confronting communicative and discourse rights and explained the need for communication because of the disparate interests created by division of labour—ultimately, the need for consensus. Perhaps more controversially, Habermas also saw society as an amalgam of lifeworld and system where lifeworld consists of the world as seen by its residents as they live their lives and interact with each other. System, on the other hand, is an intrusive factor embedded in lifeworld in which existing power structures channel human behaviour. While this concept constitutes an important contribution to sociological theory, it should be noted that it is not essential in the context of freedom of expression which is more dependent on Habermas's theories of discourse and communicative action. From the perspective of freedom of expression, the essential contribution is that division of labour creates the need for consensus which can be attained only through a communicative process. As discussed in chapter 2, respect for opinions is an essential aspect of this process and therefore restraint of hurtful speech that is contrary to the building of consensus may be justifiable.

From the viewpoint of guiding and building national laws, adding the sociological considerations not only augments the arguments for expanding rights of freedom of expression but also justifies tempering these rights with social responsibilities. The sociological approach recognises freedom of expression as just one of the rights shared by members of society. Expression is a valuable component of basic rights but so are other interests that play a crucial role in overall social harmony—the right of each citizen to be free from intrusion and harm from other members. Privacy is also an essential aspect of individuation and the social division of labour. Modern charters and bills of rights recognise that expression is just one of a bundle of rights that must be accommodated. The American federal structure implicitly recognised this balance until the state/federal balance was disturbed by twentieth-century constitutional interpretations. The federal constitution contained an absolute bar to speech restraint but permitted state constitutions to regulate speech as required by local interests. When the First Amendment was extended to the states, the balances and values contained in the state constitutions, which were being abused by the state of Alabama, were displaced by the more inflexible federal constitutional law which the Founders had not intended to displace state law. While Europeans and Canadians experiment to find the right balance, the United States, while not exactly wearing a constitutional strait jacket, must negotiate around the less forgiving language of the First Amendment.

Just as the mechanical and organic aspects of societies differ both temporally and geographically, the essential societal role of freedom of expression will ebb and flow. From the interests of society, laws must not be absolute and immutable but should be able to mirror and reflect these societal needs. While it is impossible for doctrinal laws to perfectly match societal needs and values, the closer the approximation, the better the result.

Over the past two centuries, there has developed a rich and substantial literature concerning the theoretical arguments for freedom of speech. In the first decade of the twenty-first century, Professor Samuel Nelson looked back at the theoretical network and suggested that, given the universe of competing interests and values, the freedom of speech debate had to move beyond the American First Amendment and had to take on board multiple speech justifications as well as considerations of competing values; utilising what he has termed the "pluralist framework for freedom of speech."[1] Nelson stated that the concept of pluralism, as opposed to monism, in the context of freedom of speech has three aspects:

> First, the framework is at its core value pluralist and opposed to universalist claims. No single principle can serve as an ultimate criterion or common metric for all free speech questions. While self-realization, equality, and truth/democracy all fall short as comprehensive solutions to free speech problems, the framework is open to a wide variety of values that underpin freedom of speech, including these. The pluralist framework need not be limited to these values, although such values are those most often discussed in relation to freedom of speech. The pluralist framework allows us to make judgments about competing free speech claims, but these judgments will not be made by reference to a single value that ultimately trumps all others.[2]
>
> The framework is pluralist in the second sense that it is open to multiple speech justifications. The framework's pluralism rests on the understanding that some values and preferences are incommensurable. Thus arguments based on incommensurable values are likely to conflict.[3]
>
> The framework is pluralist in the third sense that it recognizes the diversity of speaking subjects. The pluralist approach recognizes that there are always several parties to a speech act. The calculus of their freedoms will vary depending on the nature of the speech act, the relative social positions of the parties, the relationship of the parties to the speech act, and the context in which the speech act occurs.[4]

Professor Nelson further remarked that one of the benefits of the pluralist approach is that it is not constrained by the First Amendment and that pluralism is not limited to existing categories of rights.[5]

The concept of pluralism finds two applications to the discussion in the preceding chapters. First, it recognises what has been referred to as the American conundrum—that the First Amendment has become the overall master of the free speech debate in America, a purpose for which it is singularly unsuited because it was never intended to have such an all-purpose application. Pluralism is difficult in the United States as long as the First Amendment presents an obstacle to balancing competing social interests. Second and more fundamentally, the concept of pluralism provides an opportunity for sociological theory to inform the free speech debate even though the values espoused may be "incommensurable" with existing speech theory.

Nelson's three senses or points of pluralism readily accommodate the sociological arguments favouring free speech. His first point acknowledges the well-accepted viewpoint that none of the free speech theories resolves all of the questions. He ratified some of the most well-known theories and added that pluralism does not need to be limited to existing values. This is an open invitation for sociological arguments. He confirmed that no single value should trump others and that ultimately a judgment must be made. Second, pluralism accepts that multiple justifications may apply to some speech and that some of the values are incommensurable. The state of being incommensurable exists when there is not a common basis of comparison and this finds special meaning when the rather alien concepts of organic solidarity, social division of labour, communicative action, validity claims, lifeworld and system are brought into a free speech question. The concept of incommensurability recognises that values may be very different or even at odds but can still be utilised to analyse the problem.

The recognition that free speech theories can be incommensurable is significant if someone accepts that the Durkheim/Habermas theoretical models support speech but does not accept that this approach finds harmony with traditional theory. Instead, pluralism allows the sociological arguments to be freestanding or even in conflict with philosophical, political or individual reasons for freedom of speech. Sociological explanations are also accommodated by the third aspect of pluralism—the recognition that speech needs to be approached from the perspectives of people in addition to the speaker. Pluralism requires that everyone who may be affected by the speech be brought into the equation. In this respect, the sociological discussion is perhaps most at home because Habermas was quite clear that from the social viewpoint, the role of the listener was very significant.

Even if the formal concept of a pluralist framework for freedom of speech does not find wide acceptance, most if not all of its aspects already form part of the discussions though not necessarily within the clear and distinct comprehensive program favoured by Professor Nelson. If pluralism is accepted in twenty-first century free speech debate, there is clearly room for the sociological concepts to be included among the incommensurable values. In fact, the ability of a discipline outside of that of traditional free speech theory to further inform the debate supports the relevance of the pluralistic approach.

Philosophers view freedom of speech as a basic right that is essential to the moral and spiritual wellness of free individuals. Sociology provides a theoretical basis for recognising that freedom of speech also plays a critical role in maintaining the organic solidarity which holds and sustains society. But not all speech promotes organic solidarity; some speech is divisive or hateful. Viewed solely through the lens of philosophy, it may be difficult to justify restraint of harmful speech. But, when the speech is examined through the sociological lens, a different result may emerge. Pluralism allows viewing the questioned speech through a multitude of lenses and then reaching a value judgment as to whether the speech should be constrained because of other considerations.

While the terminology employed in a sociological discussion is at first blush strange and alien, it really is not particularly complicated once the jargon is mastered. Freedom of speech, long cherished as a basic individual right, needs also to be considered a basic social right belonging to and supporting society as a whole. The discussion in this book is not intended to be the final explanation but rather an invitation for further application of different sociological or anthropological theory to enliven and inform the free speech debate even more.

ENDNOTES

1. Samuel Nelson, *Beyond the First Amendment—The Politics of Free Speech and Pluralism*, 15.
2. Ibid., 143.
3. Ibid., 144.
4. Ibid., 145.
5. Ibid., 153.

Bibliography

Articles/Books/Reports

Allen, David and Robert Jensen, eds. *Freeing the First Amendment: Critical Perspectives on Freedom of Expression.* New York: New York University Press, 1995.

Anastaplo, George. *Reflections on Freedom of Speech and the First Amendment.* Lexington KY: University Press of Kentucky, 2007.

Anderson, David. "Freedom of the Press in Wartime". *University of Colorado Law Review* 77 (2006): 49.

Baker, C. Edwin. *Human Liberty and Freedom of Speech* Oxford: Oxford University Press, 1989.

Baker, C. Edwin. "Scope of the First Amendment Freedom of Speech". *University of California Los Angeles Law Review* 25 (1977–1978): 964.

Balkin, Jack. "Digital Speech and Democratic Culture: A Theory of Freedom of Expression for the Information Society". *New York University Law Review* 79 (2004): 1.

Barendt, Eric. *Freedom of Speech.* 2nd ed. Oxford: Oxford University Press, 2005.

Berger, Arthur Asa. *Durkheim is Dead! Sherlock Holmes Is Introduced to Social Theory.* Walnut Creek CA: Alta Mira Press, 2003.

Bezanson, Randall. *Art and Freedom of Speech.* Urbana, IL: University of Illinois Press, 2009.

Bezanson, Randall. *Speech Stories: How Free Can Speech Be?* New York: New York University Press, 1998.

Blanchard, Margaret. *Revolutionary Sparks—Freedom of Expression in America.* Oxford: Oxford University Press, 1992.

Blasi, Vincent, "Free Speech and Good Character: From Milton to Brandeis to the Present". In Lee Bollinger and Geoffrey Stone (eds.), *Eternally Vigilant—Free Speech in the Modern Era*, 61. Chicago: University of Chicago Press, 2002.

Bollinger, Lee and Geoffrey Stone, eds. *Eternally Vigilant—Free Speech in the Modern Era*. Chicago: University of Chicago Press, 2002.

Bollinger, Lee. *The Tolerant Society: Freedom of Speech and Extremist Speech in America*. Oxford: Clarendon Press, 1986.

Bollinger, Lee. "Free Speech and Intellectual Values" *Yale Law Journal* 92 (1983): 438.

Bork, Robert "Neutral Principles and Some First Amendment Problems", *Indiana Law Journal* 47 (1971): 1.

Bosmajian, Haig. *The Freedom Not to Speak*. New York: New York University Press, 1999.

Bosmajian, Haig. *Justice Douglas and Freedom of Speech*. Metuchen NJ: Scarecrow Press, 1980.

Bracken, Harry. *Freedom of Speech—Words Are Not Deeds*. Westport: Praeger Publishers, 1994.

Brennan, Wiiliam J. "The Supreme Court and the Meiklejohn Interpretation of the First Amendment", *Harvard Law Review* 79 (1965): 1.

Bristow, Brook. "King Solomon: Did the Supreme Court Make a Wise Decision in Upholding the Solomon Amendment in Rumsfeld v Forum for Academic & Institutional Rights, Inc.?", *Mercer Law Review* 58 (2007): 815.

Brodie, Fawn. *Richard Nixon—The Shaping of His Character.* New York: WW Norton, 1981.

Bunker, Matthew. *Critiquing Free Speech: First Amendment Theory and the Challenge of Interdisciplinarity.* Mahwah, NJ: Lawrence Erlbaum Associates, 2001.

Butler, Judith. *Excitable Speech: A Politics of the Performative*. London: Routledge, 1997.

Calhoun, Craig, et al, eds. *Contemporary Sociological Theory*. 2nd ed. Oxford: Blackwell Publishing, 2007.

Chafee, Zechariah, Jr.. *Free Speech in the United States*. Union NJ: Lawbook Exchange, (first published 1941) 2001.

Chesterman, Michael. "The Money or the Truth: Defamation Reform in Australia and the USA", *University of New South Wales Law Journal* 18 (1995): 300.

Clarke, Michael. "Durkheim's Sociology of Law", *British Journal of Law & Society* 3 (1976): 246.

Coad, Jonathan. "Reynolds and Public Interest—What About Truth and Human Rights" *Entertainment Law Review* 18(3) (2007): 75.

Cohen-Almagor, Raphael. *Speech, Media, and Ethics: The Limits of Free Expression*. Basingstoke, UK: Palgrave MacMillan, 2005.

Cotterrell, Roger. *Law, Culture and Society—Legal Ideas in the Mirror of Social Theory*. Aldershot, UK: Ashgate Publishing, 2006.

Cotterrell, Roger. *Emile Durkheim: Law in a Moral Domain*. Stanford, CA: Stanford University Press, 1999.

Cotterrell, Roger. *The Sociology of Law*. 2nd ed. Oxford: Oxford University Press, 1992.

Cram, Ian. *Contested Words—Legal Restrictions on Freedom of Speech in Liberal Democracies*. Aldershot, UK: Ashgate Publishing, 2006.

"Criminal Libel Set for Abolition" *Media Lawyer* 84 (2009): 18.

Curtis, Michael. *Free Speech, 'The People's Darling Privilege'*. Durham, NC: Duke University Press, 2000.

Daniel, Glyn. *The First Civilisations—The Archeology of Their Origins*. London: Phoenix Press, 2003.

Daniel, Glyn, and Christopher Chippindale, eds. *The Pastmasters—Eleven Modern Pioneers of Archeology*. London: Thames and Hudson, 1989.

de Tocqueville, Alexis. *Democracy in America*. Folio ed. London: The Folio Society, (first published 1835) 2002.

Deflem, Mathieu. *Sociology of Law.* Cambridge: Cambridge University Press, 2008.

Demaske, Chris. *Modern Power and Free Speech: Contemporary Culture and Issues of Equality.* Lanham, MD: Lexington Books, 2009.

Durkheim, Emile. *Contributions to L'Annee Sociologique.* Edited by Yash Nandan. New York: Free Press, 1980.

Durkheim, Emile. *On Suicide.* Translated by Robin Buss. New York: Penguin Books, 2006.

Durkheim, Emile. *Professional Ethics and Social Morals.* 2nd ed. London: Routledge, 2nd ed 1992.

Durkheim, Emile. *The Division of Labor in Society.* Translated by W. Halls. New York: Free Press, 1984.

Durkheim, Emile. *The Rules of the Sociological Method and Selected Texts on Sociology and Its Method.* Edited by Steven Lukes , translated by W. Halls. New York: Free Press, 1982.

Durkheim, Emile. *The Elementary Forms of Religious Life.* Translated by Joseph Swain. BN Publishing, 2008.

Durkheim, Emile. *Selected Writings.* Translated by Anthony Giddens. Cambridge: Cambridge University Press, 1972.

Dworkin, Ronald. *Sovereign Virtue: The Theory and Practice of Equality.* Cambridge, MA: Harvard University Press, 2001.

Dworkin, Ronald. *Freedom's Law: The Moral Reading of the American Constitution.* Cambridge, MA: Harvard University Press, 1996.

Dworkin, Ronald. *A Matter of Principle.* Cambridge, MA: Harvard University Press, 1985.

Dworkin, Ronald. *Taking Rights Seriously.* Cambridge, MA: Harvard University Press, 1977.

Dworkin, Ronald, ed. *The Philosophy of Law.* Oxford: Oxford University Press, 1977.

Dworkin, Ronald. "Lord Devlin and the Enforcement of Morals", *Yale Law Journal* 75 (1965–1966): 986.

Eldridge, Larry. *A Distant Heritage—The Growth of Free Speech in Early America.* New York: New York University Press, 1994.

Emerson, Thomas I. *The System of Freedom of Expression.* New York: Vintage Books, 1970.

Emerson, Thomas. "Toward a General Theory of the First Amendment", *Yale Law Journal* 72 (1963): 877.

Emirbayer, Mustafa. *Emile Durkheim: Sociologist of Modernity.* Oxford: Blackwell Publishing, 2003.

Epps, Garrett, ed. *The First Amendment Freedom of the Press.* Amherst, NY: Prometheus Books, 2008.

Estlund, Cynthia. "Speech on Matters of Public Concern: The Perils of an Emerging First Amendment Theory". *George Washington Law Review* 59 (1990): 1.

Ewald, William. "Comparative Jurisprudence (I): What Was It Like To Try a Rat?" *University of Pennsylvania Law Review* 143 (1995): 1889.

Farber, Daniel. *The First Amendment.* 2nd ed. New York: The Foundation Press, 2003.

Faulkner, Neil. 'Gordon Childe and Marxist Archeology'. *International Socialism* 116 (2007). www.isj.org.uk/index.php4?id=367=116.

Feigelson, Jeremy, and Erik Bierbauer. "Criminal Defamation: International Reforms Advance Against a Global Danger". *Libel Defense Resource Center Bulletin* 2 (2002): 107.

Finan, Christopher. *From the Palmer Raids to the Patriot Act: A History of the Fight for Free Speech in America.* Boston: Beacon Press, 2007.

Finlayson, James Gordon. *Habermas—A Very Short Introduction.* Oxford: Oxford University Press, 2005.

Fiss, Owen. *Liberalism Divided: Freedom of Speech and the Many Uses of State Power.* Boulder, CO: Westview Press, 1996.

Fiss, Owen. *The Irony of Free Speech.* Cambridge, MA: Harvard University Press, 1966.

Fraleigh, Douglas, and Joseph Tuman. *Freedom of Speech in the Marketplace of Ideas.* New York: St Martin's Press, 1997.

Freedman, Monroe, and Eric Freedman, eds. *Group Defamation and Freedom of Speech: The Relationship Between Language and Violence*. Westport, CT: Greenwood Press, 1995.

Gearon, Liam. *Freedom of Expression and Human Rights*. Brighton, UK: Sussex Academic Press, 2006.

Gillooly, Michael. *The Third Man—Reform of the Australasian Defamation Defences*. Sydney: The Federation Press, 2004.

Goldstein, Robert. *Flag Burning & Free Speech*. Lawrence KS: University Press of Kansas, 2000.

Gould, Jon. *Speak No Evil: The Triumph of Hate Speech Regulation*. Chicago: University of Chicago Press, 2005.

Graber, Mark. *Transforming Free Speech: The Ambiguous Legacy of Civil Libertarianism*. Berkeley: University of California Press, 1991.

Habermas, Jurgen. *Moral Consciousness and Communicative Action*. Cambridge: Cambridge Polity Press, 1990.

Habermas, Jurgen. *The Theory of Communicative Action*. 3rd ed.Translated by Thomas McCarthy. Boston: Beacon Press, 1989.

Haiman, Franklyn. *Speech Acts and the First Amendment*. Carbondale, IL: Southern Illinois Press, 1993.

Hamilton, Alexander, James Madison and John Jay, *The Federalist Papers* (Seattle: Pacific Publishing Studio, 2009).

Hare, Ivan, and James Weinstein, eds. *Extreme Speech and Democracy*. Oxford: Oxford University Press, 2009.

Hargreaves, Robert. *A History of Free Speech*. Phoenix Mill, UK: Sutton Publishing, 2002.

Harris, J. W. *Legal Philosophies*. 2nd ed. Oxford: Oxford University Press, 2004.

Hart, H.L.A. "Social Solidarity and the Enforcement of Morality". *University of Chicago Law Review* 35 (1967–1968): 1.

Hastings, Chris, and Chris Gourlay, "Gagging Law to Protect Prince Charles," *The Times*, (London), 21 March 2010.

Haworth, Alan. *Free Speech*. London: Routledge, 1998.

Hay, George. *Hortensius, An Essay on the Liberty of the Press.* 1799. Reprinted at www.fjc.gov/history/sedition.nsf/page/hay_pamphlet.

Heyman, Steven. *Free Speech & Human Dignity*. New Haven, CT: Yale University Press, 2008.

Hughes, John, Wes Sharrock, and Peter Martin. *Understanding Classical Sociology: Marx, Weber, Durkheim*. 2nd ed. Thousand Oaks, CA: Sage Publications, 2003.

Hunt, Alan. *The Sociological Movement in Law*. London: MacMillan, 1978.

Inglehart, Louis, ed. *Press and Speech Freedoms in America—A Chronology*. Westport, CT: Greenwood Publishing, 1997.

Ingold, Jon. "Free Speech Suit Settled in 'Howling Pig' Case. www.denverpost.com/fdcp?unique=1323801399977.

Jones, Robert. *Emile Durkheim: An Introduction to Four Major Works.* Thousand Oaks, CA: Sage Publications, 1986.

Kelly, John. "Criminal Libel and Free Speech". *Kansas Law Review* 6 (1958): 295.

Levy, Leonard. *Freedom of Speech and Press in Early American History: Legacy of Suppression*. New York: Harper Torchbooks, 1963.

Lewis, Anthony. *Freedom for the Thought that We Hate: A Biography of the First Amendment*. New York: Basic Books, 2007.

Lewis, Anthony. *Make No Law—The Sullivan Case and the First Amendment*. New York: Vintage Books, 1992.

Lidsky, Lyrissa. "Defamation, Reputation and the Myth of Community". *Washington Law Review* 71 (1996): 1.

Lipschultz, Jeremy. *Free Expression in the Age of the Internet: Social and Legal Boundaries.* Boulder, CO: Westview Press, 2000.

Lisby, Gregory. "No Place in the Law: The Ignominy of Criminal Libel in American Jurisprudence". *Communication Law and Policy* 9 (2004): 433.

Lukes, Steven. *Emile Durkheim: His Life and Work, A Historical and Critical Study*. 2nd ed. Stanford, CA: Stanford University Press, 1985.

Lukes, Steven, and Andrew Scull. *Durkheim and the Law*. Oxford: Basil Blackwell Publisher, 1983.

McNamara, Lawrence. *Reputation and Defamation*. Oxford: Oxford University Press, 2007.

Media Law Resource Center, "Criminal Libel Update". *MLRC Bulletin* 123, December 2009.

Meiklejohn, Alexander. "The First Amendment Is an Absolute". *Supreme Court Review* (1961): 245.

Meiklejohn, Alexander. *Free Speech and its Relation to Self-Government.* 6th printing. Clark, NJ: Lawbook Exchange, [1948] 2008.

Mill, John Stuart. 'On Liberty'. Folio Edition. London: Folio Society, [1859] 2008.

Milmo, Patrick, and W. Rogers, eds. *Gatley on Libel and Slander*. 11th ed. London, UK: Sweet & Maxwell, 2008.

Milo, Dario. *Defamation and Freedom of Speech.* Oxford: Oxford University Press, 2008.

Milovanovic, Dragan. *An Introduction to the Sociology of Law.* 3rd ed. Monsey, NY: Criminal Justice Press, 2003.

Milton, John, *Areopagitica*. Rockville MD: Arc Manor, [1644] 2008.

Mitchell, Paul. "Malice in Qualified Privilege". *Public Law* (1999): 3.

Moon, Richard. *The Constitutional Protection of Freedom of Expression.* Toronto: University of Toronto Press, 2000.

Morrison, Ken. *Marx, Durkheim, Weber—Formations of Modern Social Thought.* 2nd ed. Thousand Oaks: Sage Publications, 2006.

Nelson, Samuel. *Beyond the First Amendment—The Politics of Free Speech and Pluralism.* Baltimore, MD: Johns Hopkins University Press, 2005.

Newmark, Gideon. "The Strong Medicine of Overbreadth as Applied to Criminal Libel". *Case Western Reserve Law Review* 59 (2008–2009): 553.

Ovey, Clare, and Robin White. *The European Convention on Human Rights*. 4th ed. Oxford: Oxford University Press, 2006.

Paine, Thomas. *The Age of Reason.* (originally published 1794, 2007 reprint of 1896 ed). London, Folio Society, 2007.

Pasqualucci, Jo. "Criminal defamation and the Evolution of the Doctrine of Freedom of Expression in International Law: Comparative Jurisprudence of the Inter-American Court of Human Rights". *Vanderbilt Journal of Transnational Law* 39 (2006): 379.

Peters, John. *Courting the Abyss: Free Speech and the Liberal Tradition.* Chicago: University of Chicago Press, 2005.

Peters, Joris, and Klaus Schmidt. "Animals in the Symbolic World of Pre-Pottery Neolithic Gobekli Tepe, South-Eastern Turkey: a Preliminary Assessment". *Anthropozoologica* 39 (2004): 179.

Pickering, William, ed. *Durkheim Today*. Oxford: Berghahn Books, 2003.

Pohlman, H. L. *Justice Oliver Wendell Holmes—Free Speech and the Living Constitution* New York: New York University Press, 1991.

Post, Robert. "The Social Foundations of Defamation Law: Reputation and the Constitution". *California Law Review* 74 (1986): 691.

Pritchard, David. "Rethinking Criminal Libel: An Empirical Study". *Communication Law & Policy* 14 (2009): 303.

Rabban, David. *Free Speech in Its Forgotten Years.* Cambridge: Cambridge University Press, 1997.

Redish, Martin. "The Value of Free Speech". *University of Pennsylvania Law Review* 130 (1981–1982): 591.

Reich, Cary. *The Life of Nelson A. Rockefeller—Worlds to Conquer 1908–1958*. New York: Doubleday, 1996.

Restatement of Torts (Second) (1965).

Richardson, Elliot. *Reflections of a Radical Moderate.* New York: Pantheon, 1996.

Ritzer, George. *Contemporary Social Theory & Its Classical Roots.* 3rd ed. New York: McGraw Hill, 2010.

Ritzer, George, ed. *Encyclopedia of Social Theory*. Thousand Oaks, CA, Sage Publications, 2005.

Robbins, Ira. "Digitus Impudicus: The Middle Finger and the Law". *California Davis Law Review* 41 (2008): 1403.

Robertson, Geoffrey, and Andrew Nicol. *Robertson & Nicol on Media Law*. 5th ed. London: Sweet & Maxwell, 2007.

Rosenberg, Norman. *Protecting the Best Men: An Interpretive History of the Law of Libel*. Chapel Hill, NC: University of North Carolina Press, 1986.

Sack, Robert D. *Sack on Defamation—Libel, Slander and related Problems*. 3rd ed. New York: Practising Law Institute, 2007.

Sadurski, Wojciech. *Freedom of Speech and Its Limits*. Dordrecht: Kluwer Academic Publishers, 1999.

Scanlon, Thomas. "A Theory of Freedom of Expression". *Philosophy & Public Affairs* 1 (1972): 204.

Scanlon, Thomas. "Freedom of Expression and Categories of Expression". *University of Pittsburgh Law Review* 40 (1979): 519.

Schauer, Frederick. "The Boundaries of the First Amendment: A Preliminary Exploration of Constitutional Salience". *Harvard Law Review* 117 (2004): 1765.

Schauer, Frederick, and Walter Sinnott-Armstrong, eds. *The Philosophy of Law.* Oxford: Oxford University Press, 1996).

Schauer, Frederick. "The Political Incidence of the Free Speech Principle". *University of Colorado Law Review* 64 (1993): 935.

Schauer, Frederick. "The Role of the People in First Amendment Theory" *California Law Review* 74 (1986): 761.

Schauer, Frederick. *Free Speech: A Philosophical Enquiry*. Cambridge: Cambridge University Press, 1982.

Serafimova, Maria, Stephen Hunt, and Mario Marinov, eds. *Sociology and Law: The 150th Anniversary of Emile Durkheim (1858–1917).* Newcastle upon Tyne: Cambridge Scholars Publishing, 2009.

Shiffrin, Steven. "The Politics of the Mass Media and the Free Speech Principle". *Indiana Law Journal* 69 (1994): 689.

Skolnick, Jerome. "Foreword: The Sociological Tort of Defamation". *California Law Review* 74 (1986): 677.

Smolla, Rodney. *Free Speech in an Open Society.* New York: Vintage Books, 1993.

Starkie, Thomas. *A Treatise on the Law of Slander, Libel, Scandalum Magnatum and False Rumours*. Ithaca, NY: Cornell University Library, [1832] digitally reprinted 1994.

Strenski, Ivan. *The New Durkheim.* New Brunswick, NJ: Rutgers University Press, 2006.

Strossen, Nadine. "A Defence of the Aspirations—But Not the Achievements—of the US Rules Limiting Defamation Actions by Public Officials or Public Figures". *Melbourne University Law Review* 15 (1985–1986): 419.

Sunstein, Cass. *Democracy and the Problem of Free Speech.* New York: Free Press, 1995.

Sunstein, Cass. "Free Speech Now". *University of Chicago Law Review* 59 (1992): 255.

Tedford, Thomas, and Dale A. Herbeck. *Freedom of Speech in the United States*. 5th ed. State College, PA: Strata Publishing, 2005.

Thomas, W. John. "Social Solidarity and the Enforcement of Morality Revisited: Some Thoughts on H.L.A. Hart's Critique of Durkheim". *American Criminal Law Review* 32 (1994–1995): 49.

Trevino, A. Javier. *The Sociology of Law.* New Brunswick, NJ: Transaction Publishers, 2008.

Trigger, Bruce. *Understanding Early Civilisations—A Comparative Study.* Cambridge: Cambridge University Press, 2003.

Tucker, D.F.B. *Law, Liberalism and Free Speech.* Totowa, NJ: Rowman & Allanheld, 1985.

Walker, Clive. "Reforming the Crime of Libel". *New York Law School Law Review* 50 (2005–2006): 169.

Wallace, Ruth, and Allison Wolf. *Contemporary Sociological Theory—Expanding the Classical Tradition.* 6th ed. Englewood Cliffs, NJ: Prentice Hall, 2006.

Waluchow, W.J., ed. *Free Expression—Essays in Law and Philosophy.* Oxford: Oxford University Press, 1994.

Weinstein, James. *Hate Speech, Pornography and the Radical Attack on Free Speech Doctrine.* Boulder, CO: Westview Press, 1999.

Wellington, Harry. "On Freedom of Expression". *Yale Law Journal* 88 (1978–1979): 1105.

Werhan, Keith. *Freedom of Speech—A Reference Guide to the United States Constitution.* Westport CT: Praeger Publishers, 2004.

Williams, Robert. *The Law of American State Constitutions.* Oxford: Oxford University Press, 2009.

Williams, Susan. *Truth, Autonomy, and Speech: Feminist Theory and the First Amendment.* New York: New York University Press, 2004.

Wittfogel, Karl. *Oriental Despotism—A Comparative Study of Total Power.* New Haven, CT: Yale University Press, 1957.

Yanchukova, Elena. "Criminal defamation and Insult Laws: An Infringement on the Freedom of Expression in European and Post-Communist Jurisdictions". *Columbia Journal of Transnational Law* 41 (2003): 861.

Zeno-Zencovich, Vincenzo. *Freedom of Expression—A Critical and Comparative Analysis.* Abingdon, New York: Routledge-Cavendish, 2008.

CASE LAW

European Union

Cumpana v. Romania, decision of Grand Chamber, European Court of Human Rights, Appeal 33348/96 (17/12/2004).

United Kingdom

Campbell v. MGN Ltd [2005] 4 All ER 793 [HL].

Campbell v. MGN Ltd [2004] 2 AC 457 [HL].

Derbyshire CC v. Times Newspapers Ltd [1993] AC 534 [HL].

Jameel v. Wall Street Journal (Europe) [2007] 1 AC 359 [HL].

Liberace v. Daily Mirror Newspapers, reported in *The Times*, 18 June 1959.

United States

Abrams v. US, 250 US 616 (1919).

Ashton v. Kentucky, 384 US 195 (1966).

Brandenburg v. Ohio, 395 US 444 (1969).

Brown v. Board of Education, 347 US 483 (1954).

Buckley v. Valeo, 424 US 1 (1976).

Cantwell v. Connecticut, 310 US 296 (1940).

Citizens United v. Federal Election Commission, 558 US__, 130 S.Ct. 876 (2010).

Collin v. Smith, 578 F 2d 1197 (7th Cir 1978).

Curtis Publishing Co. v. Butts, 388 US 130 (1967).

Davis v. Federal Election Commission, 128 S.Ct. 2759 (2008).

Forum for Academic and Institutional Rights, Inc v. Rumsfeld, 291 F Supp 2d 269 (D NJ 2003), reversed, 390 F 3d 219 (3d Cir 2004), trial court affirmed *sub nom, Rumsfeld v. Forum for Academic and Institutional Rights, Inc,*547 US 47, 126 Sup Ct 1297 (2006).

Garrison v. Louisiana, 379 US 64 (1964).

Gertz v. Robert Welch Co., Inc., 418 US 323 (1974).

Gitlow v. New York, 268 US 652 (1925).

Mapp v. Ohio, 367 US 643 (1961).

Miami Herald Publishing Co v. Tornillo, 418 US 241 (1974).

Mink v. Knox, 613 F.3d 995 (10th Cir 2010), on remand, Case 1:04-cv-00023-LTB, Slip Opinion, filed June 3, 2011.

Miranda v. Arizona, 384 US 436 (1966).

New York Times Co v. Sullivan, 376 US 254 (1964), reversing, 273 Ala 656, 144 So 2d 25 (Ala 1962).

Parmeleee v. O'Neel, 145 Wash App 223, 186 P 3d 1094 (Ct App Wash 2008).

Philadelphia Newspapers, Inc. v. Hepps, 475 US 767 (1986).

Pines v. Tomson, 160 Cal.App.3d 370 (1984).

Roffman v. Trump, 754 F.Supp. 411, 415 (ED PA 1990).

Rosenbloom v. Metromedia, 403 US 29 (1971).

Rumsfeld v. Forum for Academic and Institutional Rights, Inc, 547 US 47, 126 Sup Ct 1297 (2006).

State v. Baron, 318 Wis2d 60, 760 NW2d 34 (2009).

State v. Hafer, 94 Wash 136, , 162 Pac 45 (1916).

State v. Powell, 114 NM 395, 839 P2d 139 (1992).

Stratton Oakmont v. Prodigy Services Co, 23 Media L Rptr 1794 (New York Supreme Ct 1995).

Sykes v. United States, 131 Sup. Ct. 2267 (2011).

Tollett v. United States, 485 F.2d 1087, 1098 fn 27 (8th Cir 1973).

United States v. Eichman, 496 US 310 (1990).

West Virginia v. Barnette, 319 US 624 (1943).

Whitney v. California, 274 US 357 (1927).

Wooley v. Maynard, 430 US 705 (1977).

CONSTITUTIONS

Alabama Constitution of 1901, Sec. 4.

California Constitution, Article I, Section 2(a).

Canadian Charter of Rights and Freedoms 1982.

Constitution of the State of Connecticut, Article First, Sec. 4.

Constitution of the State of Florida, Article 1, Sec. 4.

The Texas Constitution, Article 1, Sec. 8.

US Constitution, First Amendment.

Wyoming Constitution, Article 1, Sec. 20.

Legislation

Communications Decency Act of 1966, 47 USC Sec 230(c).

Coroners and Justice Act (2009) (UK) 73 (b).

Defamation Act 2005 (NSW) Sec 5 (Australia).

Oklahoma Statutes 21-774.

Sedition Act, 5th Congress, 2d Session, Ch 74 (1798).

Solomon Amendment, 10 USCA s 983(b) (Supp. 2005)

Wisconsin Statutes 942.01 (3) (2007-2008).

Wisconsin Statutes 942.03 (2007-2008).

Treaties/Conventions

American Convention on Human Rights, adopted by the Organisation of American States 22 November 1969, entered into force 18 July 1978.

Convention for the Protection of Human Rights and Fundamental Freedoms, Article 8.

Convention for the Protection of Human Rights and Fundamental Freedoms, Article 10.

Universal Declaration of Human Rights, Article 19.

OTHER SOURCES

Declaration of Independence, Paragraph 2 (1776) as unanimously adopted by the Thirteen Colonies.

Index

Made in the USA
Monee, IL
12 November 2026

e4192629-e7a8-4cf4-ab11-5acd63a7c4bcR01